Letters from Egypt

by

Mary L. Whately

Letters from Egypt
ISBN: 978-1-61634-065-0

Originally published in 1879
By Dodd, Mead & Company
New York

This edition edited by Sonya Shafer

Published and printed by
Simply Charlotte Mason, LLC
P. O. Box 892
Grayson, Georgia 30017
U. S. A.

Cover Design: John Shafer
Production Date: August 1, 2015

www.SimplyCharlotteMason.com

Contents

Editor's Note

Though written in 1879, this glimpse into Egyptian culture is still helpful and timely. For it is the older beliefs and customs that laid the foundation for what Egypt has become.

The author's insight into customs, culture, and climate ring true even today. Upon completing a read-through of this book, I picked up a modern photographic and diary travelogue from Egypt. So many of the components of the photos and comments called up a mental connection with what Mary Whately described more than one hundred years ago!

And the Scriptural tie-ins that she pointed out are amazing. You will gain a better cultural understanding of many Bible verses as you read through *Letters from Egypt.*

I have sought to keep the old-fashioned spellings from the author's original text. In the editing process I omitted some small portions that might tend to cause division rather than unity among believers, and added Scripture references to help identify the many Bible quotations and allusions that are woven throughout the letters.

It is my hope that these *Letters from Egypt* will touch your mind, your imagination, and your heart.

Letter I
Introductory

My Good Friends,

By God's providence I have been led to settle in this distant land, and can but seldom visit England; however, I do not forget friends there, for whom I always have felt great interest. One day it came to my mind that I might do some little good to old folk at home—and perhaps to the young, too—in spite of being so far off, and having a large school to look after, and several other things; and this was my idea:—that I would write some simple familiar accounts of the land of Egypt where I dwell, which might be useful and pleasant, and which might lead such as are *praying* Christians (and I believe there are many such to be found in humble abodes) to join with me in asking the Lord to let the Gospel light shine into this land where there is so much of ignorance and darkness and false belief.

There are indeed so many books about Egypt already, that some may think another was not wanted, but most of the learned and historical books would not suit any one who had not received an advanced education, and many are very difficult to understand even for those who have had this; the others are chiefly written by travellers, and being written in general by those who were ignorant of the language of the country, and who had only stayed a short time there, are apt to be full of mistakes and incorrect notions.

I have lived a great many years here, and my business has been among the people, especially the poor, and the children. I began to study the language as soon as I arrived, and am accustomed to converse in it with different classes of the people, and also to visit them and receive them in my turn, so that I can tell you a good deal about their ways and habits.

But before we begin to speak about the Egyptians of the present day we must first understand something about the country itself and its former inhabitants.

All who study their Bibles know that Egypt is there spoken of very frequently; indeed, except Canaan, the promised land, no other place is so frequently alluded to in Scripture. The first time we hear of it is in the twelfth chapter of Genesis, where we find Abraham going to sojourn in Egypt on account of the famine in Canaan, and afterwards we have the history of Joseph's captivity, leading to the settling of his family there, and the sufferings of the children of Israel under Pharaoh. There are very ancient histories and records of the Egyptians, many of which are of peculiar interest as confirming the Scripture accounts; not that the word of God *needs* the histories of uninspired man to prove its truth, but that it is very curious and beautiful to see that, the more learned men search into the records of the past, the more clearly do the accounts given in the Bible stand out. To give one instance out of many, some very old writings on stone were discovered in the ancient Egyptian characters (or picture letters), and when the meaning was, after much trouble, made out, they found it alluded to the great famine, when people from all countries came to buy corn in Egypt (Genesis 42). The old Egyptians were idolaters, and though in many things they were a very clever people, they were foolish as well as wicked in this, and made idols of every possible material; some of stone so large that they seemed to represent giants of the most enormous size; others so small that they could be carried in the pocket or round the neck, and these were often carved out of agates or cornelians, and other rare polished stones; others again were made of a curious sort of blue pottery, others of copper; they are still found in the sand in the places where the ancient people of the land used to bring their dead and have their idolatrous temples. They also worshipped many animals; monkeys, cats, beetles, were all revered, but the *bull* was considered especially sacred, because they fancied one of their chief gods had taken the form of a bull, and they kept many of these creatures in sacred enclosures, gave them divine honors, and actually buried them in coffins of polished marble, having first embalmed their bodies,—which means to wrap them up in linen with quantities of spices, and then bake, by very slow heat, in ovens. I have seen these marble coffins, and have often picked up the whitened bones of the sacred bulls in the sand, in a place where once a great city and splendid temples are believed to have stood.

The golden calf made by Aaron to please the children of Israel was no doubt made in imitation of the Egyptians among whom the people had lived so long, and of their sacred bulls: the inspired Psalmist, in holy anger at the profane and wicked action, says, "So they turned their glory into the similitude of an ox which eateth hay" (Psalm 106:20).

It is sad to think of a people so learned and clever in many respects, being so darkened in mind as to religion; for in the arts of life they were far more advanced than the nations of Europe, who at that early time were mostly quite barbarous and savage in their customs, and ignorant of much that was quite familiar to the Egyptians. While our own ancestors were living in wretched huts built of reeds, with neither books nor public buildings, and scantily clad in the skins of beasts, the Egyptians had built long before stately palaces for their kings, and temples for their idols, of solid stone, so strong that, after so many hundreds of years, a great part still remain; and though in ruins, some of the great pillars are quite perfect. They carved inscriptions on the walls of these buildings, and on pillars of granite or marble, and on the images of their gods. Their writing was very curious, consisting not of letters, as with us, but of signs like small pictures, each sign expressing a word. Some of these signs were remarkably ingenious, and showed much thought and wisdom. For instance, an eye was used as a sign of the all-seeing power of God; for it seems they had some little idea of a Supreme Power, although a very indistinct and imperfect idea. But as I have already said, they worshipped various living creatures, as well as the idols they made with their own hands. Their priests and learned men are believed to have first taught that the Divine Spirit entered into certain animals, and that others were emblems or signs of the Divine Power; and by degrees the emblems came to be looked on as real deities of an inferior order, and thus received worship.

But the bull was not the *only* animal which was honored by tombs and special burying-places, though none was so highly thought of and revered. I once visited an ancient burial-place for sacred cats, and actually saw in the pit many bundles of linen brown with age, which contained the bones of the dead pussies! These when exposed to the open air were apt to crumble and turn into dust, but when first found were in good preservation, the pit or cave being in dry sand, and the air of the country very dry and pure.

Human beings were buried in the same way, rolled up in linens with spices, and then exposed to heat, after which they were packed in cases of wood and stone.

The people seemed to have tried in this way to keep their dead from the decay which is the lot of all flesh, not knowing that *One* alone who tasted of *death* yet saw no corruption, because that holy One alone was without *sin*.

Thousands of yards of the linen for which Egypt was famous were wasted in thus wrapping dead men and dead animals. I saw an ancient tomb which had been recently opened more than twenty years ago; and lying among the sand and rubbish that had been thrown out, I found a small earthen jar without any opening to it.[1] On breaking this it was found to contain one of the sacred birds of the Egyptians called an Ibis (as I was told by a learned man who was of the party visiting the tomb). I unfolded at least two yards of half-burnt linen (for it had been baked according to their custom), and found within the crumbling bones of the bird, his long beak being quite perfect,—a memorial of the folly of man in thus wasting time and labor, and yet more their *sin*, in worshipping the creature more than the Creator.

In my next letter you will have a little more on the early history of Egypt, and some account of its climate and productions.

[1] It seems the custom was to make the jar after the embalmed creature was ready, and then to bake all, otherwise it would not have got in, as no sort of opening was to be found.

Letter II
A Little about Old Egyptians

In the Book of Exodus we read, that after Joseph's death, and that of the generation following, there arose a "*new* king who knew not Joseph." Now it is plain that this must have been a king from a distance, and not a son or nephew of the Pharaoh who was Joseph's friend, as such would not have been ignorant of the history of that remarkable person, who was second only to the monarch himself, and who had saved Egypt in the great famine. The early histories of Egypt show that there were several changes of what is called the "dynasties" or royal families of Egypt, one king being overcome and driven out by another from a distant province, or from even a different country, and sometimes the old race or dynasty returning again.

But it is not easy, even for the most learned men who have searched carefully into the records of those ancient times, to be sure of the dates or exact periods at which the events spoken of took place. We must recollect that there was no printing and no paper then, so that the records and histories were written either on stone or on skins carefully prepared, or upon the leaves of a certain reed which was used in Egypt for writing on. Only portions of their ancient writings have come down to us, a great deal having been lost or destroyed in the course of time: so it is only by putting a bit from one and a bit from another together, that learned men can find out what happened and was recorded. However, one thing is quite clear, even to unlearned people, and that is, that the Pharaoh spoken of in Exodus was of a different family and race from the Pharaoh whose dream Joseph interpreted; the name of Pharaoh was given to all the kings of the country, just as afterwards Caesar was to all the emperors of Rome. But though Pharaoh himself knew not Joseph, it is impossible that the people should not have known something of the true God from the descendants of Joseph and his brethren; and therefore they were as sinful as he was in oppressing the Israelites, and shared in the punishments sent by God in the time of Moses.

After the chosen people had left Egypt, and the wicked king and his army had been destroyed in the Red Sea, the nation still remained idolaters, though they had seen the power of the Creator and the uselessness of their own false gods,—yet so perverse is man's heart. "For the customs of the people are vain," saith the prophet (Jeremiah 10:3). We may hope, indeed, that some at least did learn to forsake their idols; but, as a nation, we know they remained the same. Different foreign powers came one after another to fight in Egypt, and to obtain that fertile land for their own rulers; the Assyrians, as foretold in Scripture, for a time ruled over the people. You will see this invasion alluded to in Jeremiah 46, as well as in other places. Later, the Greeks, under the famous Alexander the Great, took Egypt; Alexandria, on the seacoast, was founded by this monarch; and he left the country to Ptolemy, one of his four successors. The family of Ptolemy reigned for a considerable period over Egypt; and such numbers of Greeks settled in the chief towns that the Greek language seems to have been learned by many of the educated among the people, and the language of the country was written in letters imitated from the old Greek characters, so that the hieroglyphic or picture characters went out of use.

After the rule of the Greek came the *Iron* power,—the Roman,—which had nearly all the known parts of the world at one time under its strong hand. The Jews and Egyptians were alike under Roman rule when our blessed Lord was born, and when the cruelty of the tributary King Herod (who governed subject to the Romans) caused the young Child and His mother to be sent by Divine command into Egypt for a season. They still show a tree,—a great sycamore fig, under which I have sat many a time,—which the tradition says Jesus and His mother and Joseph rested under on their first arrival. We cannot tell whether it be true or not, but it is possible.

After the death and resurrection of our Lord, the Gospel was brought into Egypt, it is said, by the Evangelist Mark, but of this there is no actual proof, although it appears to be probable. Apollos, whose name is mentioned in the Epistles and Acts of the Apostles, was, as you know, a Jew of Alexandria: there was quite a Jewish colony in that city, and they had adopted the Greek language (not the Egyptian, which seems strange, but Alexandria was then, as it is now indeed, full of a mixed multitude, and having been long the capital under the Greek rule, that tongue had greatly prevailed); the Old Testament had been translated by learned Jews into Greek from the original Hebrew; and at the time when Christianity began to spread in Egypt, Alexandria was a sort of centre for education, as there were many learned men there of different nations, but especially Jews and Greeks; and many books were found there both in Greek and in the Egyptian written language, which was called the Coptic. Many copies of the Scripture were written in this. When I say "many," however, you must remember it is only compared with the *utter* poverty of nations who had no books, or hardly any; but when printing and paper do not exist, books must of necessity always be expensive and few. As time passed, the Egyptian Church became corrupted, just as was the case with the Greek and Roman Church, and as always *will* be the case when the study of the Scripture is neglected, and when ceremonies and outward forms are made of too much consequence. The ceremony—the procession, the chanting, the dress of the minister, and the *way* in which the service of God is *arranged outwardly*—being more thought of than prayer and constant dependence on Christ and close attention to the Word of God, gradually takes the highest place in men's hearts, instead of being considered as comparatively of very little consequence. Besides this, in all the Christian Churches of the time I speak of, which is called by historians the "Middle Ages," there was a great inclination to adopt many old heathen festivals and customs, with a certain alteration, which was supposed to make them Christian; from these causes, and from others which I do not wish to talk of here, the Egyptian Christians had lost much of their simple faith, and though there were no doubt some believers among them, I fear there were but few, and that very many had almost lost sight of Christ in the multitude of saints they revered and the vain ceremonies in which their religion consisted.

Their clergy had become fonder of disputing about words than of teaching the ignorant, and often too much given to luxury and grandeur. At this period (about 600 years after Christ) a new religion had begun to make a stir in the world. In Arabia, which you know is divided from Africa by the Red Sea, the famous Mohammed had arisen, and his followers were fast spreading in the East, and getting more and more powerful.

This man was originally only a camel-driver, but was very clever; and having, when on a journey into Syria (as Palestine had now got to be called), learned something of the Christian religion, and something also of the Jewish, from Jews resident in Arabia, he made a book, with the help of some friends, which was compounded of passages taken from the Old Testament, and some little from the New also,—rather in the form of allusions than of actual quotations; and to these were added a great many maxims and directions of his own. He began with a great truth,—that God is one God; for he wished to overthrow the idolatry of Arabia, and so far was right; but the addition that he was himself the prophet and apostle of God was an assertion without grounds, as you of course know. The only proof that God has sent a man to make himself inspired *head* and leader must be miracles; mere *teachers* and preachers of the already-written and revealed word do not need miraculous aid, for they appeal to God's word, which is thoroughly authenticated and proved by thousands of evidences to any one who fairly examines it. But any one who claims to be the medium of a *new* revelation is in a different position from a teacher of revealed truth, and should have miraculous powers to prove what he asserts. The Arabian prophet spoke of visions and wonders he had seen, but no witness was ever brought to prove that he had any divinely miraculous power at all. But the Scripture says, "If one shall come in his *own* name, him ye will receive"; and so it was (John 5:43).

We need not wonder at the great success that after a time followed, for not only were the maxims and regulations arranged so as to suit specially the nations of the East, and clothed in language peculiarly acceptable to them, but there was real good mixed with it sufficient to satisfy the moral craving of some who had conscience and morality to a certain degree. Besides this, it had the help of the arm of flesh which Christians are forbidden to use in spreading their religion. I do not mean that some bearing the *name* have not done so; but by their disobedience to the Saviour's plain command, and assurance that His kingdom is not of this world, they show that they are not in reality His disciples, or at the best are very weak and mistaken ones.

But the faith of Mohammed was aided by the sword from the first. Arabia was peopled in great part by wandering tribes, as is still the case, many of them having no houses but the "Bedouin's moving home," the tent, their wealth consisting in camels and goats. Numbers of the children of Midian and Esau, as well as the Ishmaelites, from whom the Arabs of Arabia proper are said to have descended, lead this travelling life. Other tribes were more settled, and had cities and villages under chiefs, who were generally at war with one another more or less. By degrees these tribes began to join themselves to the new leader, and to offer their swords in assisting to spread the new doctrines; at first only a very few joined, and those either relatives or personal friends; but after meeting much opposition, he gained a firm footing, and was regarded as the chosen of God by all his followers.

At last, after his death, his successors went on fighting their way with bravery worthy of a better cause. With their book, the Koran,[1] in one hand and a sword in the other, as one may say, they went on their conquering way till they had all Arabia and Palestine and many other countries under their sway and rule, and then at length they invaded Egypt also. The poor Egyptians were crushed under the fierce wild Arab soldiers, who gave no quarter: conformity or death was proclaimed; multitudes gave in and conformed; others, more courageous, or at least more true to their religion, fled and hid where they could. After a time, the Arab *Caleefs*, as they were called, that being the name of their kings or chiefs, ruled entirely over Egypt. The remnant of the Christians, though much persecuted and trampled on, were allowed to live; but the Arabic language was taught in all the schools, and soon became the only spoken tongue in the whole country, and the customs and ways of the conquerors prevailed in many respects. After a long period the poor country fell into the hands of yet another foreign power. The Turks, also Mohammedans, who had come from Asia into Europe, and taken from the Greeks the great city of Constantinople, had increased as rapidly as the Arabs had done in power, and had become masters of Palestine and then of Egypt also. But though their power as rulers was great, they never seem to have spread their language, nor mixed with the people of the land as the Arabs did. One reason for this is, that the Koran (the sacred book of all the followers of Mohammed of whatever nation) is not allowed by their religious law to be translated into any other tongue, and is therefore read and studied in the original Arabic by Turks as well as Arabs, and taught in all their schools. This would alone insure the preservation of the Arabic language among the people. Although the Turks still rule over Egypt, and the great part of the wealth of the land is in the hands of their descendants, and many of these Turkish families use their own tongue exclusively among themselves, still the Arabic is the language of the country, the Arab customs are those that prevail, and in

[1] This is properly pronounced Korann, with the emphasis on the last syllable, and the *k* a soft guttural.

many respects the Turk is still a foreigner, while the Arab is become an Egyptian.

This sketch, very short and very imperfect as it is, may just give you such an idea of old Egypt as will enable you to understand better what I wish to tell you about present Egypt, as I now see it, and as I have watched and observed its climate and people for many years.

Letter III
The River

The river of Egypt! that is the most important thing in respect of cultivation, and indeed the most important feature altogether, in the country we are now considering. How often it is alluded to in the Bible! Pharaoh, in his wonderful dream, saw the lean and fat cows coming up out of the river (Genesis 41),—not *a* river, but *the* river, observe; and into *the* river were the infants of the children of Israel thrown, and the young Moses saved in his little ark of bulrushes "in the flags by *the* river's brink" (Exodus 2:3). Then, later, we read how Moses and Aaron, at God's command, smote the waters of the river and turned them into blood (Exodus 7:20), and in the Prophets we find again and again mention of "the river" of Egypt (e.g., Ezekiel 29:9). It is not named; it is spoken of as the river of Egypt because it is the *only* river in that strange country. Just think how many rivers there are in our small island of England,—how many in Ireland, which is still smaller; the children in schools are often quite tired with the number of names they have to learn of all our rivers,—Thames, Severn, Trent, and many more. Now Egypt has but *one*; that one, however, is a large and very long river, and is very remarkable in the effect it has on the country. Egypt is, as you know, in the north of Africa, which of course is very much further south than Europe, and much hotter; the south part of Egypt, indeed, is very near the tropics, and there falls scarcely any rain except near the sea-coast. At Cairo, where I live, which is near the middle, there are sometimes four or five showers in the year, sometimes more, but rarely; in the upper provinces, only one or two; nothing would grow, therefore, if the vegetation depended on rain, and though there are heavy dews, these would be quite insufficient; the sun is so powerful that the whole land would be one vast sandy desert, dry and barren, were it not for the wonderful river Nile. At a certain season every year this river begins to rise gradually; it is supplied from the mountains where it has its source very far off in the middle of Africa, where rain falls copiously at a regular time of year. When it has reached the greatest height (which is ascertained by careful measurement, persons appointed for the purpose watching day and night as the time draws near), the dams which have been artificially made are cut or broken through, and the water overflows the low lands all over the country and fills the numerous canals which cross it in every direction. It would certainly overflow its banks naturally and without this artificial help as soon as the height of those banks had been reached by the water, but much of the country would then be untouched, and some lands get more water than they needed. From very ancient times the Egyptians knew how to regulate the flow and manage it so that (except on occasions of sudden and excessive rise which now and then make a flood in some places) the land should be properly watered; and their various conquerors had the wisdom to let the natives, who were accustomed to it, have the direction of their great river and its canals. It is probable that the irrigation was much more extended in old times, and that, instead of being as now a strip of cultivated land on each side of the river and sandy desert beyond—as is the case in a large part of the middle and southern provinces—the canals were more numerous and a far wider tract under cultivation. However, the canals are increasing under the present government, and the famous "sweet water canal" of Suez is alone a proof of what water can do in Egypt. When I first came here, the whole region where the modern town of Ismaila stands was nothing but a sandy waste, inhabited by gazelles and desert foxes. Now the great work of the two canals—the salt water one connecting the Mediterranean and Red Seas, and the sweet water one which conducts the Nile water—have combined to make it a delightful spot; gardens rose like magic, grapes and even strawberries grow where twenty years ago burning dry sand and pebbles lay, and thickets of feathery bamboo and gay flowering shrubs meet the eye and look the more attractive from the waste all around. "The parched land shall become a pool, and the thirsty land springs of water" (Isaiah 35:7). Would that those who labored in that wondrous canal had known the blessed spiritual refreshing of which the entrance of the water into the desert land affords so beautiful a type!

But to return to the river: its rise does not begin till summer, and during the winter it is gradually sinking and retiring. The winter of Egypt is very unlike our English ideas of that season; there is comparatively very little cold; the nights are indeed sharp, and sometimes a strong cold wind blows, but you would say it cannot be very severe when frost is almost an unknown thing. Some laborers in the country near Cairo once found a very thin film of ice, at daybreak, on some shallow water channels, and reported that the water was bewitched as it would not flow! So very rare was the wonder that none of them had ever seen such a thing before. Latterly, Europeans have introduced artificial ice, and cheap ices are even sold in the city; but this anecdote may show what the climate in winter is. The sun is generally warm at midday, and the people seek out sunny corners to sit in, especially the old; and now and then a party of laborers will light a fire of brushwood and sit round it in a field. The poor have a curious way of warming themselves in the short period of cold, which they feel especially, being used to such heat; there are no fireplaces, and fuel is dear, but in the country villages dry reeds and such light things are tolerably abundant. They will then light a bundle of these in the oven,—a large one made of mud brick is the common kind. As soon as this is extinct, which is pretty soon of course, the good woman of the house—or rather *hut*—sweeps out the embers, and the family cram into the oven and sleep! I was hospitably offered the use of an oven, heated on purpose for me and a friend by some kindly peasants, during one of our little voyages up the river, when stopping at a village on the coast during cold, stormy weather. But, in general, the winter months are delightful and healthy. All the fields are luxuriantly green; the orange gardens are rich with their golden fruit, and I have more than once spent a Christmas afternoon in an orange grove; while friends in England were rubbing their hands over the fire after returning from church, I and my party were picking oranges off the trees, and choosing a shady spot to rest in. The harvest of sugar-canes is in winter; a good deal of sugar is manufactured in Egypt, although not sufficient to supply all that is consumed; a large quantity is brought from France, but being not nearly so sweet, it is more expensive and very inferior. The Egyptian sugar, though less brilliantly white, is of a very good quality, and "goes far," as the housewives say, from its extreme sweetness. But the canes are not only used for sugar making; a great number are eaten—or rather *chewed*—to extract the juice, by the people, who are excessively fond of this cheap and wholesome luxury; Europeans seldom care for it, because the juice, which is thin and watery, with little flavor, and only moderately sweet, has to be obtained with an amount of trouble which they seldom think it worth,—the hard pith in which it is contained requiring Egyptian teeth to do it justice. As the natives of the country almost always have remarkably fine strong teeth, they find no difficulty in masticating the canes, and no fruit can be more enjoyed than they are in their season. The great bundles of sugar-cane on their way either to the manufactory or to the markets are a beautiful sight in winter, whether the larger species, of a rich purple color, with its flag-like green leaves waving about over the head of the camel who bears it, or almost smothering the little donkey; or the smaller kind of cane, called the native or belladee, which is of a delicate yellowish green. The former is more cultivated about Cairo, as being much larger and coming earlier, but some say the little native cane is the sweetest.

All the vegetables we have in summer in England are in their prime in the winter of Egypt, or in very early spring, and the green fields, in January, February, and March, are more brilliantly green with the rich clover of the country than any fields I have seen even in dear old Ireland, the emerald isle! But there are two sides to everything in this world, and spring drives away the verdure just as winter does with us, only that heat and not cold is the agent; the clover disappears, the cattle having eaten it, and having, poor things, nothing but dry food to look forward to for several months; the hot winds begin to blow, the corn rapidly gets yellow, and is reaped in April (I speak here of middle Egypt). By the middle of May, the intense heat of summer has usually set in and the fields look dry and brown,—unless watered with much labor from the canals; the very weeds, except the thistles, which seem to need scarcely any water, are withered up, and man most literally eats bread in the sweat of his brow if he has to labor in the field. For the native of the soil, I do not think that great heat is the cause of as much suffering among the poor as great cold. The Egyptian, if a *real* child of the country (for settled foreigners of Syrian, Armenian, or even Turkish extraction are far more sensitive to heat, though they may have been here for two generations or more), does not mind heat, and prefers summer in general to winter; if he has to labor hard, of course he must be greatly fatigued in the hot weather, but at any rate his family do not suffer with him. Cold falls *most* heavily on little children and aged persons, while these in the hot weather here sit in the shade of their mud walls, and as they do not mind dust and vermin, which abound, they appear happy in their way,—and certainly the comforts within their reach are cheap. Fuel and warm clothes, as you know too well, are costly, but the cucumbers and melons of summer here are cheap luxuries; and the pools of water in which the bare-legged boys are playing half the day cost nothing at all. Foreigners, however, even to the second and third generation, feel summer heat very trying, especially if obliged to be exposed to the outer air in the middle of the day. As far as possible they ought to avoid this, and to be very early in their habits, and temperate; with these precautions, the inconvenience will be considerably diminished.

In June, the heat is at its greatest height and the river at its lowest—every thing seems panting and parched; the ground is so hot that one can scarcely endure to lay a bare hand on its surface, and it appears as if one walked into a furnace if obliged to be out in any part of the day except the early morning and late evening. These are very lovely—the pure dry air seems to make every object stand out and look as if painted in rich and delicate hues, but like all earthly beauties these fair colors soon fade; as the hours advance a whitish haze of intense heat seems to settle over every thing, and (oh how true are the words of the Book of God in even the smallest particular!) then "the hireling earnestly desireth the shadow" (Job 7:2). Well may the weary hired laborer long for the shadow, which sets him free to throw himself down and rest, and bathe his burning brow in the waters of the little channel, and enjoy the comparative coolness of night. To us, indeed, it is but comparative, for in July the nights are only a little less hot than the days. When September comes the suffocation seems increasing, a sort of still breathless heat prevails: this shows the river is at its height. The water is not good to drink at this time, unless carefully filtered or boiled; the peasants do not, however, take this trouble, and drink it as it is. At last, about the fifth or sixth of September (sometimes several days later), the great day comes when the Nile is cut. The watchers who for a week or more have relieved each other night and day, measuring incessantly to ascertain the moment the right height has been reached, give the news, and immediately the dam is removed and the water flows; not all at once all over the country, but at first over the lower lands, and then, entering the canals, by degrees waters all the country.

All the coasts of the river are at once flooded, of course, and the effect on the landscape is wonderful to see. Where you saw yesterday a great brown dry field, reaching from the high-road all the way to the river-banks, is now a shallow lake glistening in the sun, the little villages with their groups of palm-trees peeping out like islands from the water. The pools and brimming canals look very beautiful and refreshing after the long, sultry heat; not that it is less hot, rather I think more oppressive in some respects, but the moisture is something delightful to look at; and every one is so happy. The poor women, who had to toil along a weary way to fill their great pitchers, now laugh and sing as they trip down to the water-course close at hand; the children spend most of their day in the river or the canals,—occasionally, however, getting drowned therein; the great buffaloes stand up to their horns in water, giving contented puffs to show their enjoyment; everywhere reeds and rushes spring up with wonderful speed; water birds sport in the places lately full of dry clods and choking dust; the brilliant kingfisher darts after his prey in the deep pool that was but yesterday a pit "wherein was no water" (Genesis 37:24). It is impossible not to rejoice over the inundation, and while thanking the Giver of all good for His mercies, the Christian adds an earnest prayer that the water of life may flow also in Egypt.

Then the water begins to subside, and the laborer goes out to sow his seed. Often he is seen throwing it on the surface of a shallow lake, reminding one of the words, "Cast thy bread on the waters, and thou shalt find it after many days" (Ecclesiastes 11:1). Perhaps still oftener we see the seed flung on a sort of thin mud, the man with difficulty finding a spot just raised enough to be sufficiently dry to support his weight while he stands. Raised pathways border all the canals and most of the fields that are liable to overflow, but the sower has sometimes to descend from this causeway to reach distant parts of the field. In that hot sun the water dries very quickly, and in a wonderfully short time a beautiful green hue appears spreading over the whole country. A little later the crops are in full beauty. The fields lately so bare are now all covered with rich verdure. The ancient Egyptians not unreasonably made September their new year, as after the inundation the commencement of vegetation seemed more like spring, and more suited to starting afresh, as it were, than any other period. The chief crops in Egypt are wheat, barley, beans, lentils, maize, cotton, sugar; the clover I have already mentioned, and a great variety of vegetables, as tomatoes, black and white egg-plants, cucumbers, melons and gourds, onions, garlic, and some others not known in Europe, all grow abundantly; indeed, with proper attention and plenty of water, almost any thing will grow in this fertile land. But it must be cultivated with care; not a wild berry is found that could give nourishment, however imperfect, to man; all land not made to pay its tribute by labor and watering soon becomes a sandy desert from the power of the sun.

Letter IV
The Gardens of Egypt

I have told you in my last letter something about the cultivation of this country; but you may like some further information, and especially, I think, the way in which gardens are managed here will interest you. After what you have heard about the river and its inundation, you will easily suppose that there must be a great difference between field and garden cultivation, since, if the river at the time of the overflow were suffered to flood the gardens, much of their crops would be destroyed, and the flowers and shrubs swamped and injured. Now and then, by accident, this does happen in gardens near the river. I recollect a pretty, though somewhat rudely managed garden, chiefly planted with pomegranates, on the banks of the Nile, where I once sat for an hour with a beloved friend; the year following I was at the same spot,—no garden was visible. I looked about in amazement, and said to a man whom I recognized as one we had spoken with last time, "Where is your garden gone?" He replied, "In the great flood last autumn the water washed away every tree, not one is left;" and then he went on to ask after the sick lady who had rested under his pomegranate-trees. Ah, she too was gone, but, as I told him, to that place "where the tree of life is blooming" by the heavenly city (Revelation 22:2).

But to return to our gardens. They are watered by small channels only a few inches wide, which are made to intersect or cross and recross the garden, the beds between them being usually square in shape. When they are to be watered, the gardener removes with his hand or his foot the small dams made of earth rudely heaped up at the corners, and lets the water from the well (or canal) fill them up until the level of the bed is reached. He then stops the flow by pushing the heap of earth back again, and damming up the water. Each bed gets its share in turn, generally every second, or, in *cool* weather, every third or fourth day is sufficient, so that one portion of a garden is watered every day; in very hot weather, if water is abundant and the garden full of flowers, it may be daily watered. Many gardens are dependent on wells which, with very few exceptions, are brackish and unfit to drink, but answer fairly for watering plants, though sweet water wells are more esteemed, of course.[1]

Others have water brought from canals supplied by the Nile, and the garden receives its water by means of machinery, without which it would not be possible to fill the small channels. The simplest of the machines in use is the "Shadoof." A long pole is sunk close to the well, and a large stone, as a weight, is hung to it by a rope; the other end of this rope is tied to a sort of dipper made of leather, which a man keeps emptying into the trough that supplies the channels, as fast as it gets drawn up by the weight which pulls it as soon as he looses his hold. He has to keep pulling and emptying incessantly, so that it is very hard work, though much quicker than if he had to draw up a bucket with a windlass, as we do in wells used to drinking, etc. The other machine most commonly used is a Sakea or Sahkea;

[1] Figs from certain villages that possess sweet water wells fetch a higher price in the market.

it is much less simple, but does more work in a short time. It consists of two wheels of great size, one of which is deep down in the well, and is turned by the other, the upper wheel being turned by an ox, buffalo, or camel (the former are the commonest). The lower wheel is furnished with a set of rude earthen pitchers fastened by ropes of palm fibre all round it. As fast as one half of them are filled by the turning of the wheel, the other half empty their contents into a stone trough which supplies the channels that water the garden. The sahkea is always raised a little above the garden level, so that the water easily flows into it. Very refreshing is the sight and sound on a warm day, for trees are almost always planted near it, so that the laborer and beasts of burden may have a little shade; and the trickling and splashing of the water, the sun shining on the bright drops as they fall from turning pitchers, and even the creak, creaking sound of the wheels, are all pleasant in this climate; they speak of coolness and moisture, and every one likes to sit beside the troughs and watch the flow of the little channels. The favorite tree to plant by a sahkea is the sycamore fig alluded to in several places in Scripture. It affords excellent shade from its thick foliage; the rounded leaves of rich dark green grow in such a way as to form almost a roof over one's head, and the lower branches stretch out and spread downwards, often extending quite across a path or road. You recollect Zaccheus, whose short stature hindered him from seeing Jesus in the press, and how he climbed into a sycamore-tree in order to see Him (Luke 19). When I first saw these trees in Egypt, I at once perceived how well they were suited for such an object, and that of all trees this was the most likely to be fixed on from being planted by a road for the sake of shade very often, and from its peculiar growth making it so easy to climb quickly.

We also read that the prophet Amos was a "gatherer of sycamore fruit," before called by the Lord to warn and rebuke the people and their rulers (Amos 7:14). You may like to know what these fruits that Amos gathered were; they are still largely consumed in Egypt, and probably in Syria also, but chiefly by peasants, as they do not reckon among choice fruits, and strangers generally think them disagreeable. You will remember that there is no resemblance to our sycamore of England,—it is a different tree altogether; it is allied to the fig, which its fruit is very like in shape, and it has the same peculiarity of the flower and fruit being in one. The appearance of the sycamore fig, when ripe, is very pretty; it is then of a delicate pink or salmon color, and grows either on the trunk or on the branches of the tree, to which they are fixed by such very short foot-stalks as to look at a distance as if they actually grew on the surface of the trunk. At the season, which is from the end of May to July, a man climbs the tree with a basket, which he lets down to the women who come in troops to purchase from him and retail in the town; and when the rustic baskets they bring are nicely lined with green leaves, and the pink fruit piled upon them, and placed on the head of the peasant woman, they look very tempting and pretty; but if you tasted them, you would own to the truth of the proverb, "appearances are deceitful," for any fruit more insipid and worthless I never met with.

The mulberry is often planted by the Sahkeas also; it grows to a great size here, and affords delightful shade, but the fruit is very inferior to the black mulberry of Europe and Syria; it is the white variety that is cultivated here, but very little silk is made, though I believe the white mulberry is generally planted with that view, as its leaves are thought best for silk-worms.

The ground near the water-works is often devoted to patches of onions, cucumbers, and such things as need a great deal of water, and on the low lands near the river, in many places, there are large fields of melons of different sorts; the most esteemed is called the "shamam," and is one of the most delicious of fruits, and, coming in the driest and hottest part of the year, is specially valued. What a sign of God's goodness to man is it, that just when the people crave for something fresh and cool, and when the water of the Nile is at its lowest, and often not pleasant to drink (without much filtering), the land should bring forth in abundance these juicy fruits! There are many inferior kinds, which are excessively cheap, and within the reach of the poorest in their season. A little later come the enormous water-melons. But all these belong more properly to field than garden cultivation; the melons especially do not answer well, except near the river, and in a wide space generally.

The gardens of the wealthy are often enclosed by stone walls, and latterly by iron railings, in the suburbs of the city; but the old Egyptian style of paling is usual in the country, and with all who are not able to afford expensive enclosures. It consists of the tall strong reeds so plentiful here, which, when cut and dried, form very good palings, tied with palm-fibre ropes, crossways. They need renewing after a few years, indeed, but are easily procured. These reeds are one of the great features of a real Egyptian garden, being used whenever small sticks are wanted, wood being scarce, and the native shrubs and trees often useless for "sticking," on account of the sharp thorns belonging to most of them; a reed is indispensable to the gardener in many ways, and it often makes a shepherd's pipe or flute, on which they play a monotonous but not unpleasing tune, as they keep their goats or sheep.

But the reed is capable of proving treacherous; if leaned on too carelessly giving way suddenly and inflicting a sharp wound. The prophet Isaiah alludes to this when recording the words of Rab Shakeh, the great general of the Assyrian king, who came against Hezekiah, king of Israel, "Lo, thou trustest in the staff of this broken reed, on Egypt; whereon if a man lean, it will go into his hand, and pierce it: so is Pharaoh, king of Egypt, to all that trust in him" (Isaiah 36:6). I thought of this text one day, when noticing my gardener's hand bound up; I asked what ailed him, and found that he had been driving a reed into the ground to support a plant, and it had suddenly broken and entered his palm, making a wound rather troublesome to heal.

The garden here is specially fertile in suggesting texts of Scripture to the mind of any one who makes that blessed book his study, as all Christians ought to do. Who can see the laborer opening the little channels to let the water flow over the parched earth on his beds, and returning the clods to their place with his bare foot, without recalling the words of Moses in describing the promised land to the Israelites, who had so long sojourned in Egypt that they knew no other manner of cultivation: "The land whither thou goest to possess it is not as the land of Egypt, where thou sowedst thy seed and wateredst it with thy foot, as a garden of herbs" (Deuteronomy 11:10)?

Who can see the gardens of the peasants, full of leeks and onions and garlic, and fail to remember the Israelites in the desert longing for these juicy vegetables, to which they had been accustomed (Numbers 11:5)? Truly it pleases God sometimes to let His chosen ones be for a season deprived of some things which are not sinful in themselves, and of which the deprivation is trying; but they may take warning by the Israelites, and pray to be kept from murmuring, and if He keeps them in a desert and withholds the onions and the cucumbers, He will give the manna from heaven, which is better.

You must not suppose that gardens here have no flowers in them; although, except in the cases of very rich men's gardens, the flower cultivation is not attended to as it is with us; if it were, in so fair a climate, where almost everything will grow with care and *water*, they might have an extraordinary abundance and variety. Still, they love flowers, though lazy about cultivating them, and especially prize such as are fragrant. In ordinary gardens the flowering shrubs and a few annuals are strewn, with little order, among the vegetables and fruit-trees, and some trees with beautiful blossoms are planted in all gardens of any pretension. The luxuriant growth in so fertile a soil makes this careless arrangement of no consequence; in fact, it is prettier, in many respects, than a more formal trim garden. The creepers, of which they have several native to the country, as well as some of foreign race, grow in a rich tangle round the reed fences, and the jasmine and rose, which continue in bloom more than two-thirds of the year, grow beside the egg-plant and tomato, and the effect is almost as if they grew of themselves. Annuals, if once sown, and succeeding well, become self-sown, and grow like wildflowers ever after; and then the profusion is so lovely as to make up for a little disorder. The Bahmea is a favorite vegetable here, which is met with both in gardens and in fields, and might well pass as a flower, being very pretty. It is a sort of mallow, the blossom of a delicate straw-color, with a dark brown centre. The seed-vessel is the part eaten; it is full of a glutinous juice, and is by most people esteemed highly. But the king of plants and trees in Egypt is the date palm, which is found everywhere; by the roadside, in the courts of princes' dwellings, and by the hut of the peasant, in the city, and in the village, is the graceful feathery foliage of the palm-branch to be seen standing out against the clear blue sky of noonday, or the golden and crimson hues of early morning and sunset. By the river-side, above all, great plantations of palms are quite a feature of the country. No garden is considered complete without a few palm-trees, and at least one or two are always planted when a garden is laid out.

Pictures, or rather prints, in our magazines and cheaper books, are very apt to make a confusion between the cocoa-nut palm of India and China and the date palm of Arabia, Egypt, and South Syria; I have, indeed, seen some prints representing a fabulous sort of palm-tree between the two! They are, as every gardener who has seen them in hot-houses well knows, very different, though both are of the palm-tree family, which is a large one. The cocoa-nut palm, I may observe, will not grow at a distance from the sea greater than fifty miles, or thereabouts, I believe. So, in the interior of Egypt it would not thrive if planted; but it might grow by the sea-coast, and may some day be introduced, as many Indian trees have already been. The date palm is, however, a native of the country, though much cultivated, as the fruit of the wild ones is not esteemed. Like all the palm family, its age is noted by the rings, or rather notches in the trunk, which increase every year; its branches grow from the top in a sort of feathery crown; the leaves, long, narrow, and pointed, are of a lightish green, changing with the air and the time of day more than is the case with any other tree; sometimes it looks quite a dull, dark, grayish-green, and then again almost purple, and then a golden green, and many other shades which charm a painter's eye. The flower is of delicate cream-color, and bursts out of a green sheath about a foot and a half, or more, in length; a shower of lovely little blossoms hang down from slender foot-stalks in a great cluster, something like *ivory* carvings, being exactly the color of fine ivory; when these drop off, tiny green dates appear, and gradually increase in size till they turn of a rich golden yellow or a bright red, turning as they ripen to a purplish red or a dark brown before they get dry. There are many varieties, differing somewhat in size and color. Each tree bears from seven to ten of these clusters, occasionally even more, and each cluster, or bunch, is so large and heavy that a fine one is about as much as a man can lift! The fruit is much liked by the people in its fresh state, though, in general, Europeans think it too dead sweet at that time. I was amazed to find that the poorer people will eat the date in its green state, when its astringent flavor is so intense that how they can swallow it without choking is strange. I was once persuaded by a poor woman to taste one; she had a basketful, and assured me they were very nice; I made the experiment, but never repeated it, nor can ever forget the effect upon the throat and tongue.

The date harvest is quite a feast among the people, especially country people, and village mothers choose that time to visit married daughters in town, and take them a cluster of dates as a present. The mother of one of my scholars, who has a dozen fine palms in her garden, once sent me one, and it feasted all the family and the girls of our little home, besides making several jars of preserve. The leaf-stalk of the date palm is greatly used in Egypt for making frames of all kinds, hampers, bird-cages, rustic seats, and bedsteads, and many other useful things are composed of them; and the leaves are twisted into mats, baskets, etc., but they are *not* used (as I actually saw it asserted in an English magazine that they *are*) as *umbrellas*, for the good reason that being slender narrow leaves, growing on a long stem, they would be as unfit to exclude the rays of the sun as any thing could possibly be; indeed, the shade thrown by palms is a *light* shade, not sufficient for protection from sun even when growing, unless a number are quite close together. Probably, the writer was confounding the date palm with some other species of which the leaf is wide, but this shows how careful we should be in speaking of what we have not seen or accurately ascertained to be true.

The banana is another plant very common in Egypt, and which is wild in many parts of Africa, and probably is a native of Egypt; therefore, the whole country, except the actual desert, is so under cultivation that it is difficult to know exactly what was wild once in it. The broad leaves of the banana, of a beautiful rich green, make it an ornament to a garden, and wherever water is plentiful it is planted, for its fruit is greatly liked. It has two distinct blossoms on one stem, a large reddish-brown one, somewhat of the shape of a huge tiger-lily, and, above that, a set of small white blossoms growing from the top of the flower-stem. When these drop off, a bunch of green fruit, the size of almonds, appears, and rapidly swell till larger than an egg (unless of the small variety, which is longer and thinner than the other). As they ripen they turn of a delicate pale-yellow, and are very delicious in flavor. One curious thing about them is, that they flower and fruit nearly all the year round, though the chief abundance is in autumn; but there is hardly any part of the year when some are not to be seen. As they need a great deal of water and good earth, they are not much cultivated by the peasants; perhaps they dislike the extra trouble, but they bring so good a price in the city, that I often wonder more are not planted near the canals, etc. The banana is not a tree, properly speaking; its stem is like a gigantic reed, being hollow in the upper part of the middle, and the bark is composed of pith, full of a glutinous sap. The fibres of this bark are very tough, and are used as *bass* is with us, to tie up plants, etc. When cleansed they are *fine* as well as strong, and can be made into paper of an excellent quality.

The orange (which I have already mentioned as common in Egypt) is not a native, but was introduced from other countries,—some kinds from India, as the shaddock, etc., and the common sweet orange from Portugal; it is therefore generally known as the "Portugal." I have seen in some orange-gardens eight or ten varieties of this delightful tree, all covered with fruit in different stages of ripeness; the soil suits it so well that it grows far better than in India, as I have been told by those who have come from thence, and in the end of autumn and winter oranges are both abundant and cheap, and far more juicy, of course, than those which come to us by sea. In a large garden occupying no less than ten acres (some miles distant from Cairo) I saw lemons of extraordinary size, and citrons, oranges of all kinds, and limes, all in such profusion that the boughs of some trees had to be supported, and the ground was strewn with fallen fruit. The gardener told me it belonged to a wealthy childless widow of Turkish race, who never even came to see it, and the golden splendor was seen by no eyes save those of this poor laborer, in his ragged blue shirt, and his children, and an agent who came now and then to order the sale for his lady, and doubtless to secure a goodly share for himself. It was not like one of the grand gardens of noblemen's houses in England,—no hot-houses (they would be needless in so warm a climate), no pattern beds, with varieties of choice flowers, nor even the neat gravel walk and orderly modest beauty of a humble though cheerful English garden; but yet it was lovely, very lovely in its own way, and that suited the climate better than a more formal one, though they might have had more flowers certainly, but then the creepers,—the luxuriant jasmine and orange-blossoms perfuming the air, and the vine and fig growing as if at their ease! Altogether the effect was very pleasant. We told the gardener something about the Garden of Eden, and man's first life, that interested him, and read him some texts out of a pocket Gospel, and he said how much he wished the school we talked of was nearer, that his little girl might attend it.

In this, as in every Egyptian garden, the pomegranate bore a place; its brilliant scarlet flowers were not then in blossom, but the curious and pretty fruit was still hanging on many of the boughs. The quince, plum, and apple are also cultivated in Egypt, but the two latter seem to require a cooler climate to reach perfection, as they are inferior to ours. This may, however, be merely want of knowledge in the gardeners.

It may be supposed that, in a climate so dry, the people are very fond of sitting out of doors, and few gardens are without a shady trellis or arbor, covered with vines or with some of the numerous creepers of the country. One of the prettiest of these is called, in their tongue, "The Lady of Beauty." It has a luxuriant dark-green foliage, and a pretty lilac blossom, not unlike a large bind-weed in shape. It is suited for arbors, as being of rapid growth, and insects seem not to like it, which is a great advantage. A species of perennial bean, with a pretty purple flower, is also frequently used as a shady creeper; another with a very elegant seed-vessel, like a small green bag or purse, is called the "judge's mouthful," or "bit,"—a sly allusion to *bribery*, or stopping the mouth of justice with a *purse*, being apparently intended. There is a sort of gourd, which is a pretty creeper, sometimes called the wash-plant, because its fruit consists of a kind of *pith*, which, when freed from seeds and dried, is very useful in washing, better than any washing-glove, flannel, or other invention of man's making.

But it would take too long to enumerate all the interesting and curious plants I have seen here. Before I leave the subject, however, I must tell you of a singular festival connected with gardens. On a certain day in spring, called by the name of "Smell the breeze,"[1] every one goes to a garden if possible, if not, to a green field, as early as can be. The proper thing is for an onion to be taken and *smelt* the first thing in the morning, and then thrown out of the window. Many have abandoned this old custom, but they all retain that which followed it, of spending great part of the day in a garden, carrying about flowers, or branches of trees even if no bouquet is to be had. This festival seems evidently to be the remains of the ancient Egyptian worship of the vegetable kingdom, for they considered the onion to be the king or chief of vegetables. The feast as now kept is common to both Moslem and Christian, and they do not know that their ancestors worshipped plants, most probably, but keep it up as we do some old customs, merely by tradition. The roads and fields on this day look very pretty and cheerful, with the crowds of people all in their best clothes, the women and children generally as gay as tulips, in lively-colored prints, or silks if they are wealthy; by six o'clock, and even earlier, all are out of doors, and few of their festivals seem more enjoyed or are so pretty as this.

[1] *Poetically* translated, the words would mean "Inhale the Zephyr"!

Some of the great men have lately been improving their gardens by introducing some European seeds to add to what was already known, and they succeed beautifully with proper care. I saw not long ago in a princess's garden what might be called a *wilderness* of sweet peas, for instance, and so with many others; and some modern arrangements in the way of tools are also beginning to be used. But when foreign gardeners are brought over they must have an Egyptian to look after the watering; for, if ignorant in some things, they fully understand this, which after all is the most essential business of all in so dry a climate. No scientific wisdom, no careful weeding or pruning, no watching against hurtful insects, or bringing seeds from afar, would avail to make the garden "bring forth and bud," unless plentifully supplied with water, and unless the gardener knew how to arrange the little channels, so that every spot should have its due share; otherwise fairest blossom would soon wither and the most fruitful trees perish in the burning sun.

Now does not this make a beautiful comparison to the necessity for the Holy Spirit in our hearts? Whatever of learning or wisdom we may possess, however amiable in natural disposition, however we may reason, and even heartily try to do good and put away evil from ourselves or others, we never can really prosper in our souls,—there can be no fruits of holiness *enduring* and real, without God's Spirit flowing into our souls. The "living *water*" that Spirit is called by Jesus himself, and we can no more do without that living water than the garden can do without earthly water. And the emblem is perhaps more *striking* here than elsewhere, because we *see* the water flowing in, and the vegetation so rapidly increasing wherever it comes, and the burning sun destroying with equal rapidity where it does not. The seed is the word of God, and the Holy Spirit the water which causes that seed to bring forth good thoughts, good words, and good deeds. "Thy soul shall be as a watered garden," says the prophet, "and thou shalt not sorrow any more" (Jeremiah 31:12). The second part of this blessed promise is not *yet* fulfilled (as we all too well know!), not while we live in a world which is so full of trouble and grief; but it *will* be fulfilled one day for all the Lord's people; the time is coming when they will not sorrow any more, and meantime, even among the many trials of life here below, if they trust Jesus and the work of the Holy Spirit, the *Comforter*, according to His own promise, their soul "shall be like a watered garden"!

Letter V
The People

We now come to the people of Egypt. I will not at present speak of the foreigners, of whom many are settled in the largest cities (as Cairo, Alexandria, and Suez); a mixed multitude indeed they are, and we must speak of them in due course; but the natives of the land claim our first and chief attention. They consist of two great divisions, the largest by far being the Moslem Egyptians, who are the descendants of those who conformed to the faith of their Arab conquerors, mixed with those conquerors, and became one race. The smaller division is that of the Coptic Egyptians, who are the remnant of the old Christians who did *not* conform, and who formerly were much persecuted and crushed down in many ways, their language forbidden in the schools, so that it became a "dead language" (which means one not *spoken*, but only found in books), and were forced to wear a peculiar dress, and harassed in many ways. But since the days of the famous Mohammed Alee (that great Pasha who made Egypt so nearly independent of Turkey), these severe laws were repealed, and in the present time they enjoy quite as many advantages as their fellow-subjects of the State religion. Mohammed Alee had great talent, and had the rarer quality of good sense, at least in this matter, and gave religious liberty to both Jews and Christians, and was repaid by the increased prosperity of his kingdom.

There is not the liberty enjoyed by the British subjects in Egypt, nor is education in any thing but its infancy, as one may say, as yet; still there is of late years a great movement in favor of the spread of instruction in various ways. The Khedive has been always extremely liberal towards foreigners who endeavored to establish schools, and also opened several on a large scale for giving gratuitous instruction to a number of the young of both sexes, as well as military and medical colleges. But you will like to have a little idea of the *people*, rather than to enter much into these things; and to know something about their appearance and habits, and daily life. For these letters are written especially for you who stay at home, or whose longest journey is a trip to some large town in your own country. Many of the wealthy can visit Egypt by steamer and railroad, and, from the windows of a great hotel, see more than I can describe, in less than half an hour. However, it is *only* a picture after all, whether to the real eye or to the "mind's eye," that any one can get who has not tarried long enough in a place to know the language and habits of the inhabitants, and it takes a good while for one of our northern race to do this. How strange the crowd of African faces look to one first landing on the African shore! and yet stranger sound the words of the unknown tongue, with its gutturals and curious blending of syllables together! It seemed to me like a beautiful and curious but confused dream, when I first stood on that sunny shore; wearied and sea-sick with a stormy voyage, and bewildered with the noise and shouting of so many voices all unintelligible, and so many dark faces, and having to step aside to avoid being knocked down by a string of huge camels, heavily laden with sugar-canes (neither of which had I ever before seen)—yet in the midst of confusion, and dust, and ragged children, and wretched huts, and other things far from beautiful in themselves, there was such a *light* over every thing, such a clear brilliant sunshine, and an air so balmy and soft, every thing white looked so dazzling and every color so bright, that I admired all I saw, in spite of the confusion.

It used to puzzle me very much at first to hear the people of Egypt commonly spoken of as *Arabs*, when I knew they were not from Arabia, unless a certain portion, who, as I said before, are mixed more or less with their Arab conquerors. Of course the mass of the people are an African race, but the Arab language has so completely driven out the other that the word is now commonly, though not very correctly, applied to all speakers of Arabic.

But some persons in England have a vague sort of idea that every real African must be black or nearly so, and this is a great mistake. There are plenty of negroes in Egypt, whom you shall hear about in another letter, but they are not Egyptians. The Egyptians are much darker than English people indeed, and, in the southern provinces, the peasants and all who are exposed to the sun are almost mahogany-colored; but the town people (especially ladies, who are never in the sun) are much lighter in complexion, and in the northern parts of Egypt the citizens in general are not much darker than the natives of the south of Italy and Spain, and many not at all so, indeed. All the Egyptians, if of pure race, have black hair and eyes, or so very deep a brown as to appear black at a little distance. When not affected by the malady, so frequent here, of ophthalmia (I mean when their eyes have not been permanently injured by attacks of it, as is often the case), the Egyptians have generally fine eyes; some of the peasants, who are more strong and vigorous than towns-people, are remarkable for the brightness of their eyes and the long black eyelashes that shade them. But the number who have lost one or both eyes is considerable; the poor, as they are apt to neglect the care and medical aid which are absolutely necessary, are of course the worst sufferers, and many infants lose their eyes or have them injured for life merely through the dirty habits of the mothers: but the disease is peculiar to the country, and foreigners are by no means exempt. Pure air and sanitary regulations, however, diminish the evil, and careful attention to cleanliness also does much to lighten it.

In point of teeth, Egyptians are better off than most Europeans, having white, even, and strong teeth, with rare exceptions, and I have often seen quite aged persons able to eat a plateful of nuts without the least difficulty and without using any *nut-crackers* but those in their heads! The women of the working classes, who are a great deal in the air and carry burdens on their heads, have very good figures, straight and upright, and walk well; they have usually rounded arms and well-turned wrists, and the feet and hands small and neat in shape. But the women who, from being more wealthy, do not need to work out of doors, etc., are generally shut up very much in their houses, and from an inactive life become fat and shapeless while still in their prime.

The peasant farmers are generally fine-looking men, active and well knit, and frequently of a good height; but the townsmen are less healthy and much oftener undersized. The artisans, who are active enough indeed, are sometimes sturdy fellows; but the shopkeeper is much less on the move than an English shopman, generally serving his customers without rising, and having all his goods in a little den close round him, and heaped up by his side; it is not strange, therefore, that he should be sallow and unhealthy in comparison to those who take exercise.

From the outward appearance of feature and complexion we naturally come to dress. I am sure my female readers will open their ears at this, and one may whisper to another: "Do let us hear what they put on in those distant parts!" The climate of Egypt is for so great a part of the year very warm, that the tight cloth garments of European men are certainly very unsuitable, and when I first came here no one *but* Europeans ever wore them. I really cannot find out why they have latterly come to be worn by most of the highest class of men, and by the Government officials and servants: their dark skins make them look very ill in black or dark-colored clothing, and the weather makes it a punishment to support them; yet, except for wearing a small red cloth cap instead of a hat, the European garments are the fashion in that rank of life. The mass of the people, however, still adhere to their old dress; the merchants, tradesmen, and many others of the towns-people, wear a very becoming garb, well fitted to the climate; of course it varies according to the means of the party, but the poorer tradesman has much the same shape and style, only substituting cotton for silk, etc. Properly, then, it consists of an outer coat of fine cloth, fitting easily to the shoulders and back, and descending in graceful folds to a little above the heels or ankles; being cut in what the dressmakers know as *gores*, it is not so full as to be cumbersome and heavy; this is open in front, and displays an inner garment of striped silk, also long, and girt round the waist with a wide sash of strong silk or embroidered cotton. In the house, unless the weather be cold, the outer coat, or "gibbeh," as they name it, is laid aside. This inner dress is, like the outer one, worn of a variety of colors, but generally two shades of the same are chosen with remarkable taste; a dark purple outer coat, for instance, would be worn with an inner one, or "kaftan" as it is called," of light purple, with a white or black stripe; a dark red, again, will have a "kaftan" of delicate crimson and white stripes; and a dark brown, a cinnamon-colored one, with a stripe of cream or pale yellow, and so on. Slippers of red or yellow leather, made extremely wide and comfortable, instead of pinching the toes as European shoes so often do; and a turban of white muslin, or thin calico, wound round a red cloth cap, which it almost conceals, completes the real old Egyptian gentleman's dress. You must observe that a *turban* is in the East a special mark of a *man*; when he dies his turban is placed on the bier, and a turban is carved on the entrance to many tombs. The idea that dressmakers used to have,—and I am afraid some ignorant painters also,—that a turban was part of an Eastern *lady's* dress, is so very absurd that it would make an Oriental laugh, as *you* might if he were to describe Dame Smith as going to church in a smock frock and corduroys instead of her bonnet and cloak. But to return to our Egyptians. The peasant and the workingman, who cannot afford such rich garments as I have described, nor would be able to do their active work in them, wear much simpler ones; a blue or white cotton "kaftan," not unlike our old-fashioned English smock frocks, only much longer and fitting better to the figure, with a waistcoat of colored print fastened with a great many white cotton buttons and loops, worn inside, but showing in front, is the dress of the laboring-men; short cotton trousers and a shirt are worn inside by all, except young children or the very poor; and a "rough garment" of goats' or camels' hair, or rough twisted woollen, often spun by his own hands, is always worn in winter by the country-man, to whom it serves as a blanket by night and a covering by day, if the wind be cold, or if he is heated by work and wishes to rest. You may recollect the passage in Exodus 22:26 and 27, "If thou at all take thy neighbor's raiment to pledge, thou shalt deliver it unto him by that the sun goeth down: for *that* is his covering *only*, it is his raiment for his skin: wherein shall he sleep? and it shall come to pass, when he crieth unto me, that I will hear; for I am gracious." How beautifully is here shown God's care for the poor, whose rough mantle was his only blanket!

The women are always veiled when out of doors, unless those of the poorest class, who are less particular, and merely draw the end of their dark muslin mantle over the lower part of the face if a man is present; I have frequently seen a woman whose hands were occupied hold down the covering with her teeth till the man or men had passed by, which has a very droll effect in European eyes. But the proper dress for native Egyptian women is a long strip of black silk, or rather a species of crape, which is light, and yet not transparent; it is woven on purpose from the outer coating of the silk cocoons, or inferior part of the silk; this is fastened on by a curious little tube of either gold or brass, which supports it, a sort of fillet being tied round the head with the tube and veil attached, so that when put on the whole face is hidden excepting the eyes, which peer out above the black veil in a mysterious way, as it seems to strangers. One of *white* muslin is worn by ladies latterly, in preference; but all alike hide the face from the age of twelve, and, in wealthy families, much earlier. The peasant girls in the country are not so early hidden, and usually remain with their faces free until they marry (which, however, is generally at a very early age), and they are much less careful about veiling than in towns. The poorer women, and all, whether rich or poor, who live in the country and are the wives of laborers or farmers there, wear a loose dress of dark blue or black cotton or linen (occasionally cotton and silk, if it be the wife of a well-to-do farmer). A large mantle of either very dark purple, black, or blue and white in a very small check, with broad stripes of dark blue, and sometimes of crimson, at the edge, and with a fringe all round it, is the out-door garment; this answers instead of shawl, hat, cap, pelisse, or cloak; a flowing veil of thin black muslin being worn inside, and the outer mantle laid off in the house, or while they are at work. No belt or sash is worn by the peasant women, who, on account of having often to work in great heat, are accustomed to have their clothes all loose, as a night-dress with us. Even in winter they have no change except a small waistcoat, or sleeveless jacket, of red or yellow cotton print. Full trousers, tied just below the knee and falling over to the ankles, are worn instead of petticoats by all the respectable classes:[1] but the poor are frequently able only to afford a single garment. In the great heat of summer they require less clothing, of course, but the veil and mantle seem, though often ragged, to be quite essential for every woman. Little girls are often seen with only a little blue or white shirt on, and occasionally, in hot weather, with nothing, and boys very often. If they possess two suits of clothes they will put on one over the other for warmth in winter; I have seen a woman who had, she told me, *three* entire suits one "a-top of the other," as you would say, and this accounted for her looking so remarkably stout.

The citizen's wife is differently attired; she always wears a

[1] These are often in prints and pictures represented as *fastened* round the *ankle*, which is quite incorrect.

large mantle of thin black silk for her out-door dress, which entirely hides her figure; and within it she has another silk garment, a sort of gown, without sleeves, tied round her waist with a sash; this dress is yellow, pink, or any bright plain color she likes. As this is rather an expensive dress, it is only the rich who can often renew it; the rest wear the same for years, till the silk is rusty and threadbare, but on no account will they substitute any other material, unless in the case of very young girls, who wear a mantle of plain white calico. The in-door dress of the women of the middle and upper classes is very pretty, and suitable to their climate. It usually consists of a print or colored muslin dress, or one of white, in hot weather; very simply made, without flounce or ornament, the neck and sleeves only being trimmed if the wearer likes. When going out visiting, and on festivals (especially weddings), dresses of brocaded silk, etc. are worn by all women who can afford them, but the style I describe is that usually seen even among wealthy persons. In winter, a coat or jacket of warm material is worn, and ladies often have these of cloth, either lined with fur or embroidered with gold thread. A muslin handkerchief of delicate colors, with a little silk border made by the needle, is worn on the head by all who keep the real Egyptian costume,—the hair in long plaits hanging from under it; but some ladies have not adopted the less pretty and more fantastic head-dress brought from Constantinople, made of gauze, fastened over a *stiffening* of some kind, and ornamented with artificial flowers. The tight high-heeled boots brought from France are also beginning to drive out the simple and convenient shoes of the country, which, being very easy, were more suitable for a hot, dusty climate. They are, however, still worn by thousands, and those who have given them up are repaid by suffering with tender feet, etc.

The Egyptian ladies live a very retired life, not being allowed to go out of doors freely as we do in England, and many never get beyond the walls of their house at all (which is, therefore, an actual prison) unless to go to the public female bath, and on rare occasions to visit near relatives; some have not even this degree of liberty, and have only the change of air to be had in going from one room to another. But before taking a peep into these secluded abodes, we will first see what is the life of the humbler classes, who, as in every country, are by far the majority of the people.

Letter VI
The People (continued)

The difference of the dwellings of those who earn their daily bread in our country and in Egypt is very great. I do not of course mean that we have not, unhappily, in great cities miserable abodes enough,—garrets, cellars, and plenty of wretched buildings. But the greater part of the inhabitants of those comfortless homes are such as have been reduced by some special cause, and in a very large number of cases the cause is vice, idleness, or intemperance; in others, wasting sickness or accident to the head of the family, etc. These garrets and cellars are not the *national dwellings* of the country, even for the very poor. The white cottage, with its thatched or tiled roof, is the proper "countryman's" dwelling in England, and however poor many of such cottages are, they are very, very far superior to the village homes of Egypt.

The mud hut *is* the national abode of the working classes of Egypt, and the great mass of the people inhabit huts. The villagers, of whom we shall hear more particularly afterwards, are not the only ones who live in little huts; many are found in certain quarters of the towns, and always in their suburbs. A cow accustomed to a tolerable stable would decline living in one of these; yet they are the habitation, not of the vicious, but of the respectable poor man, and probably are just such as his forefathers dwelt in, from the days of Pharaoh down to this time. Mud, roughly tempered, is the only material, and the roof often consists of a bundle or two of reeds; sometimes a beam or two, with a little dab of mud on the top; no window, a door so low that the owner can lean on it as he stands, and neither whitewash nor furniture within;—generally so small that the wonder is how the family get in, not that they have no furniture, for there would not be room for it.

A few stones outside the door answers for a kitchen; a cooking pot or two, a mat, and generally a box for those who have any thing worth keeping, is the whole of the contents, and too many have not even these. Press, shelves, clock, and such comforts, are not heard of; a wadded quilt rolled up in a corner is often found in those who have some little means, but not with day-laborers in general. It is not the poor over-taxed peasant's fault that he has little to make a house pleasant, nor does he feel the need of comfort, not being used to it; the hardship is very much less than in a cold climate, since by choice the natives of the country of the working-class sleep out of doors great part of the year, and live outside nearly always. Still they are within at times, the women more than the men, and, if they were not so neglected and ignorant, would know that, however humble, a place *may* always be made clean; the dirt, dust, vermin, and disorder in the dwellings is what makes their great misery, much more than small size and poverty. They might take example by the numerous bees which find their living from the fields of clover all around the cities in the springtime. What is more fragrant than the fresh honeycomb, or more perfect in cleanliness and neatness than the little cells made by that wonderful insect? Not Egyptians *only* might go to the bee for a lesson, as you will, I dare say, agree with me. The town houses of the poorer people, which yet are not *huts*, but are two-storied or more, and built of mud *brick*, and not mere sun-dried mud worked in a mass, are not as superior as might be supposed, from this same want of order and cleanliness, and, as they contain a little more, I think they are almost worse. The women are married as mere children generally, and have never been taught clean and orderly ways.

Many decayed and ruined houses in Cairo and also in Alexandria have been lately removed; this was by the order of Government, and a very wise order it certainly was, but unless the new houses be kept clean, they will soon fall out of repair, and be as bad as the old.

The discomfort and dirt in the poor peasants' dwellings is not, you must observe, the consequence of *drink*, as is sometimes, alas! the case in English homes, where people ought to know better; it is sheer ignorance, added to the laziness which in hot countries is more natural perhaps than in colder ones (though I think we all know a few lazy folks even in cold places)! Our poor young Egyptian mother has not the least idea that dirt brings disease to young children, for instance: her mother, and her grandmother, and her mother-in-law, and old aunts and cousins without number, all tell her that nothing is so *unlucky* as to wash baby. So she never *does* wash him; he rolls on the mud floor half naked, and, when he can toddle, often entirely so; or, if still very young, is wrapped in her veil and popped in a corner while she picks the corn and kneads the bread. A cradle is met with in all the better class of houses, but the laborer's child is cradled in *mud* either in-doors or out, as the season suits. With the abundant space they have—for their villages generally occupy a great deal of land—they might build better abodes, and might make shelves, etc. in what they have, but it never seems to enter their heads.

I once gave a poor Coptic peasant, who could read, a copy of a Gospel, which he was very glad to receive; but a year afterwards, on asking him about it, he told me (with evident regret at the accident) that the sheep had eaten it! A great fat coffee-colored sheep shared his small hut with himself, his wife, and five children, and having neither shelf nor drawer nor closet, he could not keep even a book from the creature's rapacious appetite! I gave him another, which he put in the bosom of his blue kaftan, declaring neither child nor sheep should ever get at it!

Countrymen know the absolute necessity of regularity in tilling the ground, and laborers are very steady in watering and sowing at the right times; and the women, more disorderly in their ways, yet generally keep to the right time for fetching water from the canal or river (with so clear a sky they need no watch to tell how near is sunset); but in every thing except cultivating the soil and milking cattle, their life is very irregular: women will be up before dawn one day and very late the next, especially in town, where they have not rural business to force them to rise with the light; they sleep in their day clothes, and rise without brushing hair and washing,—at least, far the greater number evidently do so. On festivals, indeed, they go to the bath and have a grand "cleaning up," but meantime even decent peasant women will leave their hair, in its many little plaits, untouched from week to week, aye, and month to month!

The meals are as irregular as the sleeping, except the last; the family assemble for supper about sunset in summer, and a little later in winter, when the days are shorter, because the chief meal for most Egyptians is the supper, and it must, of course, always be so for any who have to work in the fields at a distance from home. But the rest of the day they seem to take some bread when hungry, and eat it, squatting down in a shady corner in summer, and a sunny one in the cold weather, with a bit of water-melon or some dates, or by itself, as may happen to be convenient. The children scramble about with whatever they can get, in dust-heaps, or on the wall, or in the hut, as they like, dirt and liberty being supreme. Those of a more respectable class, though not taking their meals as you would, or in what you would call a comfortable way, are a good deal above this half-savage style of living. They assemble, such of the family as are at home, at *some* hour in the forenoon; and if the father of the house be absent, his dinner is sent to him, or he has a dish from a cook-shop, if convenient.

I remember once visiting the wife of a Coptic priest in a small country town; of course, they did not live in a hut, but a good house. I *cannot* say it was *clean*, but it only needed cleanliness and neat order to have made it a cheerful, though modest dwelling. The good woman spread a wadded quilt over the mat, with one or two hard stuffed pillows, and we sat down and had a pleasant and friendly talk together, her sister and herself being intelligent persons, although without any education, neither being able to read, or even knowing the alphabet. This was nothing unusual, however, as no woman in the whole town knew a single letter. Presently, the eldest girl brought a small round table, only a few inches from the ground, and set on it a tray with the family dinner, or breakfast (the first regular meal of the day it was, but, being ten o'clock, the children at least must have eaten before, I fancy). It consisted of some eggs slightly fried in a great deal of butter, in a metal dish, and a saucer of coarse earthen-ware, containing a piece of native cheese, which we should call cheese begun and not finished, being in fact only *curd* drained and slightly salted (it is good when freshly made, but does not keep very long); the bread was in dark, thin, round *flaps*, and was laid in a heap on the tray, and then distributed round; no plates, forks, or knives were used, each taking with the fingers and a bit of bread, portions of the eggs, etc. A pitcher of water, with a narrow neck for drinking, stood beside them, and all sat round the table on the floor. They cordially invited me to share, and, of course, I took a morsel not to be impolite, although I had breakfasted some time before, in a way more suited to my habits. After the meal, which was quickly over (for people do not care to linger over cold water as they would over a cup of tea), we fell to talking again, and I could not help reflecting, while turning over the leaves of the Testament I had with me, what a delightful thing it is, that, however different we may be in our customs,—in the bread we eat and our way of partaking of it,—the bread of life is the same for all, and suits all alike! We may share that bread joyfully with every fellow-believer, or even every one who shows the least wish or intention of becoming such; the differences are but trifles of earth that are to pass away, but the "one Lord, one faith," are for ever. Why will not the hungry in soul come to Jesus to be fed when they *have* heard of Him, and listen to the blessed words He spoke,—"I am the bread of life"?

Letter VII
What They Eat

In the last letter I told you about bread, but you will like some more particulars, I think, and also something about the other articles chiefly used as food. Bread is the staff of life as with us; it is not here as in many parts of India and China, where rice takes the place of bread; they are fond of rice, and eat more of it than we do, it is part of the diet of every tolerably comfortable family, but it is not so cheap as to be within the reach of the poor except on occasions. When, for instance, I have a house-cleaning, or any business giving extra fatigue to the out-door servants who are called in for the time to help, they expect a dinner or supper afterwards, consisting of boiled rice with some melted butter mixed with it and a little pepper and salt, and think this a capital meal. But bread is their daily food, with some relish or other, according to the season and means. Every family makes its own bread; there is a good deal, indeed, sold in the streets, chiefly on palm frames carried on a boy's or woman's head, and "cried" about, especially in the morning and at sunset; but this is chiefly used by travellers, or workmen without a regular home, or on occasion when the home supply is short, etc. No family above a beggar's will use it constantly and daily. To eat "street bread" is to be at the last point of discomfort with an Egyptian. They do not buy the flour, but the wheat, and as this has been threshed by the oxen treading it out upon the ground, it is always full of bits of earth and dust (it is said, indeed, that some is put in by fraud on purpose to increase its weight). The cleaning of the corn takes up a good deal of the woman's time, and then it has to be carried, usually on the head of the housewife, unless she is able to keep a servant or slave, to the mill; and when ground, has to be sifted, for, the chaff not being separated in the grinding, that and the bran are sifted out together, which is not a good plan, as no one can make what we call whole meal bread. When sifted, the women bring leaven, or sour dough, which they use instead of barm, or yeast; and, when it is risen sufficiently, work up their dough, making it very moist, *slack* as bakers say, and beating it up much more than we think necessary; often they are at it in the middle of the night, if it is risen so as to be ready, and will spend two hours in beating and slapping the mass, producing quite a loud sound with their hands. When finished, it is made into very small round cakes, or flaps, each of the size of a small plate; these are stuck against the sides of the oven, and baked in *less* than a minute each, but so many are needed that the process takes some time. A hundred loaves of this size is not too much for a family of two grown persons and two children in a week, so it may be supposed what a business it is to prepare bread for a large family; however, the fuel needed for this sort of bread is not much, as the thin loaves so soon get done. This kind of bread, or something resembling it, is used in Syria also. It is more easily *broken* than *cut*, and as other food is all partaken of with the fingers (soup only excepted), it would not occur to Oriental servants, in laying a table, to provide a knife for cutting *bread*. I make this remark because some persons have a fanciful idea that there is some special meaning or *sign* in our Lord's breaking instead of cutting bread at the Last Supper, when He gave it to His disciples as an emblem of His body to be soon broken for them and for us. We know that, literally and accurately speaking, His body was not broken, but rather cut, pierced, and wounded, and that it is expressly said, "A bone of Him shall not be broken" (Psalm 34:20; John 19:36). The word evidently means only that He was wounded, and suffered in the flesh for our transgressions' sake, so that whether we break or cut a piece of bread in our celebration of the Lord's Supper is a point of no importance, any more than is the kind of bread; the real essential is that we should remember our Lord in that holy and comforting service, and think of all He suffered for us, and that He is the true Bread that came down from heaven. I dare say you recollect the Gospel parable where the man asked his friend to lend him three loaves of bread, because a traveller was come to see him, and he had no bread in the house to set before him (Luke 11:5). Now in many parts of the East *three* loaves is, to this day, the portion usually placed before a single visitor when his host wishes to be sure he has enough. Unless extremely hungry, he would hardly need more than two of the ordinary loaves, but it would be thought mean to set *less* than three before him, and in a wealthy family they send in a whole *heap* of loaves; but our Lord's illustrations are, for the most part, relating rather to the humble classes than to the rich and great; and I remember being struck, formerly, with hearing a lady say to her servant, when another person's servant had come on some business, "Carry the man a plate of dinner and three loaves," and I was often afterwards reminded of the parable.

The Egyptian bread is seldom relished by Europeans,

who generally make their own, and in the cities Greek and French bakers are numerous. But when cleanly made and quite fresh it is not to be at all despised; the disadvantage is that it is very bad to our taste when *stale*, and very quickly gets hard and dry, especially in summer.

The diet of the people is usually frugal as regards the middle and poorer classes, but they manage to have a greater variety than people of similar means in England, and, I think, in this they are right, as a change of diet is more wholesome than to eat almost always the same things. All the cheaper vegetables are taken, as they come in season, by all except the very poorest, and very few there are who cannot obtain cucumbers and melons in their most plentiful time; the latter are often sold in slices, which are to be had for the smallest coin extant, and are, no doubt, very refreshing to weary laborers or ragged boys in the heat. The lentils so often named in Scripture are a great article of food in Egypt, and are very superior to the vegetable of that kind in France, which seems an inferior species. The Nile boatmen chiefly live on a thick soup made of lentils, with onions and hard bread broken up in it. Probably this was Esau's famous pottage (Genesis 25:29–34), the lentils being, when shelled and uncooked, of a bright reddish orange color (the text says "that *red* pottage," meaning made of red lentils. Jacob was in the act of preparing it, no doubt). It is very savory and good, and a highly nourishing diet. Tomatoes, egg-plants, black and white, and various gourds are abundant, as well as many vegetables more familiar to you. Some of them are made into stew or soup for supper (with a little meat for those who can afford it), others are eaten raw; and fruit is often eaten with bread as a meal. At other times, salted curd, or pickled turnips, etc., are taken as a relish, and the Egyptian beans are a favorite breakfast with all;

rich and poor alike enjoy this simple and wholesome dish. The beans require to be slowly cooked in a great earthen jar, which is usually done by the seller, who puts it in hot ashes for several hours; they are sold in the early morning by plates-full, and seasoned with a little lemon-juice and salt and pepper, and the addition of a morsel of butter makes them an excellent article of diet.

In winter and early spring, when milk is tolerably abundant, even in towns, a preparation of milk, made sour and thick, is very popular, and is sold in small earthen saucers, making a favorite supper.

The Nile produces a good deal of fish, which the people living near the river can procure cheaply enough; but in the warm season it ought to be cooked almost as soon as caught. It is inferior, however, to sea fish.

The allusions to parched corn in Scripture are frequent, and this is still a favorite dainty in Egypt as well as in Syria; but in the present day maize is oftener used than wheat, for although I have often seen the *reapers* eating parched wheat, which they made by roasting the ears in the field, I never recollect seeing it sold in the markets, whereas maize is one of the chief street cries at its season under the name of "Durra." Probably it took the place of parched barley or wheat after its introduction (as is generally supposed, from America),[1] the larger grains making it more suitable for parching than any other; but that alluded to in Scripture must have been either barley or wheat. We see there that parched corn was looked on as a sort of rustic treat, which country folks sent to their friends; David's father sends "parched corn" as well as cheeses to his sons in Saul's army

[1] Some still think, however, that it was a native also of the East. I leave antiquarians to decide.

(1 Samuel 17:17), and the friend of the prophet Elisha sends him "full ears of corn in the husk," evidently for parching (2 Kings 4:42); and just so do friends in the East now send, or bring, a basket full of corn in the husk for their town relatives to enjoy. In harvest-time we often see the reapers lighting a little fire of chips or sticks in a field and roasting the ears over it to prepare this simple but much relished luxury, and such scenes bring to mind the sweet story of Ruth and the parched corn that she brought home from the field to regale her mother-in-law, "when she had eaten and was sufficed" (Ruth 2:14–18). For though that history took place in Syria, the ways and habits are in a great many things the same in Egypt.

As we might suppose, from the many allusions to it in Scripture, *butter* is very much used in the East. Some learned men indeed have thought that sour milk or curds was meant by the word translated butter; but I can bear witness to the fact that it is much *more* used in cookery both in Egypt and Syria than in England,—I mean in larger quantities, and that many of their dishes, otherwise very good, are made too greasy to suit most English palates. But they rarely use it as we do on bread; it is generally boiled down and clarified, and thus kept in jars. In the country villages here, they eat it sometimes on bread in winter, but little is eaten fresh, comparatively.

The way they make butter in Egypt would strike you as curious. A prepared goat skin is half filled with milk, slightly sour, and then hung to a peg driven into the wall, or to a post, and a woman, taking hold of a long string tied to it, pulls it to and fro, with a jerking motion, till the butter comes. She then drains the lumps, but neither washes nor salts them in general. So, except in quite cold weather, it soon gets rancid; but very little is made in the hot season. In early spring, when the cattle are fed on clover, is the butter time, and quantities are then made and clarified for summer use. The favorite dish, without which no feast would be complete, and which is the staple in most families above the poorer class, is rice cooked with this prepared butter, as I observed before. At their festivals, both Copts and Moslems make cakes, which are often so rich with clarified butter as to crumble in lifting them unless taken with great care. The peasants can not afford to make theirs so very rich, nor (luckily) to make themselves bilious with such diet very often; but they do not think it a real feast in Egypt (or Syria either) unless it be "a feast of *fat* things" (Isaiah 25:6). Here, again, the Bible allusions are fully carried out.

But while eating articles literally soaking with butter, I have heard an Oriental in a very dignified position, who had visited England, speak with almost a shudder of slices of bread and butter which had been offered him! An *Egyptian* would not have been so much surprised, it would only appear to him a sort of homely, rustic thing, to eat "fresh butter with bread," as peasants do in spring in his country; he came not from Egypt, but Syria.

The quantity consumed is, however, as before observed, greater than with us, no vegetables being ever cooked merely with water. Meat is used in smaller quantities, and generally mixed with vegetables, unless on occasions of a feast, when a roasted lamb is sometimes served up, or a large joint. At weddings a great deal is spent on feasting, as we shall see when speaking on that subject.

Letter VIII
Superstitions

You will not be surprised to hear that the Egyptians are full of superstitions. Most, if not all nations, the mass of whom are ignorant, are superstitious. In England, when there was less education than in the present day, numbers of silly superstitions prevailed, particularly among country people; and even some who should have known better were yet so foolish as to hold fast to the nonsense they had been told in their childhood by ignorant persons, and were afraid to sit down to dinner if thirteen were present, or of spilling a pinch of salt, meeting a magpie, and other equally ridiculous things. I knew a lady who was afraid to change a dress, accidentally put on the wrong side out, because it was "ill luck," as she pretended. A wise friend asked her, "Who is *luck?* Is he a god that you worship him?" She was much vexed, but still clung to her folly. If such things are found in a professedly Christian country, we cannot wonder that they should abound here, and they *do* to a sad extent. Not that all alike are under the dominion of fear that superstition brings. Some are naturally cheerful, and do not think about the future much; others are sensible, and see how foolish these fancies are; but the greater number, particularly of women, are complete slaves to superstition, and though they declare they believe in one

God, yet *practically* they believe in a great many. The chief of all their objects of fear, however, is what they call the evil eye; more frequently they speak of this unseen but dreaded power, simply as "the eye." It *appears* to mean a sort of envious and grudging feeling on the part of some person or persons who look at their child, or property, or any thing of value. But there must be a deeper meaning than this, since, however unkind the envious neighbor might be, unless he or she did actual mischief out of spite, no harm could be conceived to follow from his envy except to his own wicked heart. But a passing stranger, who never again sets eyes on the child, or animal, or whatever it may be, or a neighbor, who is known never to have lifted a finger against them, are equally supposed to be the medium of conveying the injury which they attribute to this terrible power. It seems to me to be just a horrid fiction invented by the father of lies in order to draw away people's minds and hearts from God, for strangely enough, though invoking Him frequently on other occasions, I do not ever recollect hearing them *pray* to be protected from this supposed power. No,—some odd and foolish trick or charm is to be used to *balk*, as it were, the evil influence. One of the commonest is a sooty mark or *dab* on the forehead of a child. One often meets a little girl or boy with this mark, usually one of the richer class; the mother puts on this disfiguring sign to divert, as she fancies, the power of the eye, because of the extraordinary beauty of the child. I have seen it quite as often on very common and even plain-featured children as on pretty ones; but, of course, every mother thinks her *own* something wonderful; it is just because she happens to be of an anxious temper that she marks it.

A Coptic mother, who was visiting at my house the other day, had a little child with her who struck me as being even more untidy and dirty than was usual (and I am sorry to say a neat-looking child is still rather an exception here); but the mother being very well dressed and not poor, the coarse peasant's frock of rough blue cotton, and the shaggy, filthy hair, did look singular, and I took occasion, when she made some remark about his delicacy of health, to say something in favor of cleanliness, "especially in such hot weather." "Ah! but do you know I have lost several" (I think she said four) "children, and I keep this one coarsely dressed and dirty on purpose: it is that he may live." I felt sorely inclined to say, More likely that he may *die*. The poor, foolish woman continued, pointing to her boy, who was a small and by no means a very pretty child, "He is, as you see, so *lovely*, it is best to keep him *thus*," nodding mysteriously to imply that to make him as unattractive as possible was the only chance of his escaping the evil eye.

Another, a very pleasant woman, and one not insensible to the Gospel, dressed her baby in black from head to foot, even his little cap being of black calico, because she had lost two or three before, and a friend assured her that to make him a "little monk," as she expressed it, and dress him in black for a term of years, would be a sure means of preserving him. The dear little thing was taken, however, and the poor mother was candid enough to confess she had been wrong. She was a professing Christian like the other, but Moslems equally believe in the evil eye.

A very common defence (or *fancied* defence) against their *fancied* danger of the eye, is to hang charms around the neck or waist of a child, or tie them to its little cap.

These charms consist of leather rolls or bags, or else tin cases, in which are enclosed papers, with verses of Scripture written by a priest on them if the child is a Copt, or from the Koran if a Moslem. Whether *really* written is doubtful, but they never open them to ascertain it.

Thought oftenest seen on children, they are also worn by some grown people; negroes and Nubians, in particular, are very fond of them, and wear them tied by a thong of red leather to the arm above the elbow, where it is easily seen when, for the convenience of work, the long sleeve is stripped and tied back. A Coptic woman, who, having had some little education and some knowledge of the Bible, should have known better, was once persuaded by a priest to let him prepare her a charm against certain headaches from which she suffered; whether she thought they came from the evil eye, or not, I am not sure; the fact was, they were simply bilious headaches, which strict diet and a few doses of suitable medicine afterwards cured. However, she was persuaded to try the charm first, and paid a sum she could very ill afford for it: the priest had no idea of writing a few words on a strip of paper for nothing. She was at last convinced by one of my family that this was a very foolish thing, and if the paper really was, as it professed to be, a Psalm of David written out, it could do no possible good by being applied to the outside of her head. She agreed to open it, and lo! it was no Psalm at all; nothing but a few letters without meaning and some *scrib-scrab*. She was heartily ashamed, and, I hope, never used charms again. Those whose eyes have been opened so that they have received the Gospel in their *hearts* have often opened these paper charms and always found nothing but a little *scrib-scrab*; but it matters nothing in reality whether the verse of Scripture is there or not, as when *so* applied the Bible itself is, in the sight of the Almighty, no better than a mere scribble.

I have seen young children so laden with charms in tin cases that they could scarcely support them without inconvenience when crawling, or toddling about; yet it is seldom one can induce a mother to remove them, so deeply are these superstitions rooted in the hearts of the people. For a certain kind of weak eyes, a red coral or bit of cornelian is hung by a thread from the head so as to dangle over the eye. I asked what possible good this could do, when first observing it on a scholar, and the teacher told me (evidently in doubt as to the thing herself, but inclined to think it worth *trying*) that the red color of the stone was supposed to divert the redness from the eye. I think medical advice is more frequently sought for bad eyes, so terribly common here, than formerly, but still many continue to prefer charms and to think that till seven days have elapsed after being attacked no one should apply any medicine for ophthalmia, and in bad cases blindness, either partial or total, is sometimes the result.

I once called on the mother of a scholar and found her with one eye tied up, and offered to look at it, saying that if a simple case, perhaps some of the eye-water we always kept might be of service. She refused to lift the covering, and seemed angry at my request, which was certainly not made from curiosity, as I saw too many bad eyes in Egypt to be curious about them, and the sight is a very unpleasant one; but she did not understand that only sincere kindness could make the offer, and the teacher who was with me explained that she thought it was a case of evil eye on *hers*, and that keeping it from *any one's* observation for a certain period was her only chance.

Another still more singular case is that of covering a baby's face that the eye may not *strike* it, as they say. I have often heard of such, and one occurred in the family of an old servant, who himself told me that he had not seen the face of his little grandchild, though it was then some months old. "You see, my daughter lost several," he said, "and she fancies it is the evil eye. I tell her to trust in God, but" (shrugging his shoulders) "these women,—what is one to do with them? Her mother, and aunts, and all, will have it that it is 'the eye.' " This poor babe had its face hidden from every one except its father and mother, and what was more, from the fresh *air*, by a thick black handkerchief, till it was a year old; and then, you will say, did they at last take it off? God did it for them. He took the poor infant away, and I feel no doubt its happy little spirit sees light in Paradise through the love of Jesus, though it never saw the light on earth. For the family, who were Copts, lived in the Coptic quarter of Cairo, and at that time, before the late alterations in some of the streets, it was a place where the sun could scarcely penetrate, so dark and narrow were the lanes, and when—*if ever*—the child was taken outside the house, it was under cover of its thick black veil. Still, though in a miserable, bungling way, it was dedicated to Christ, and prayed for by the old man; and the arms of the Saviour reach *far*, especially to catch up the little ones.

Another, and I think a worse, case was one of a woman, also a professing Christian, and of the same family, who, after losing two children, sent, on the arrival of the third, for a sort of witch or "wise woman" ("foolish woman" would be a more suitable name), who came to stay for some weeks in her house, and *every* time a visitor called—and in this country all the female neighbors, friends, and relatives call on these occasions—this woman performed incantations and burnt incense to dispel the effects of the possible evil eye from some one of the guests. I would not go to see her, though an old acquaintance, on hearing this, because it seemed to be a sort of devil worship, as when I next saw her, a good while after, I plainly told her.

She tried various other charms, one of which was disgusting enough, bathing the infant in the blood of a pig! It followed its little brother and sister, and for aught I know the poor silly mother may be trying the same experiments on another, unless the Lord has seen fit to open her eyes, and teach her to trust in Him.

A very common charm is to hang a stuffed crocodile (procured from Upper Egypt, for there are no crocodiles near Cairo) over the door of a newly-built house. Sometimes an aloe plant is put up instead. No doubt one is as useful as the other.

Animals are supposed to be as easily *struck* as children; and indeed, in old times in England, some people used to fancy that if a cow suddenly ceased to give milk she was bewitched, as they expressed it, and poor old women were accused of this crime, which they *could* not commit even if they wished to do so. We need not then wonder that the poor Egyptian peasant woman who has a fine cow will frequently prevent any one from seeing her. I remember one being quite angry when I asked leave to send my servant to bring the milk she sold us. "No, no, I don't let any person in while I am milking," she said. "Why, if any one saw me milking, my cow would most probably get 'the eye,' and give no more. My cow is a very fine one; I let no one see her that I can help, and always keep the stable door closed at milking time." Horses and camels often have charms hung round their necks to protect them, as is supposed; but as it is not universal, I imagine *all* do not put trust in this nonsense.

It is curious how ready people are to take trouble in the wrong way and the wrong place (not in Egypt alone, indeed). The worry they give themselves about these charms I have mentioned, and the trouble and often *cost* of getting them, if used in another way, would really rid them of much evil, or diminish it. For example, I once was visiting in a respectable and rather wealthy Mohammedan family: a young married woman was sitting with me, sister-in-law to the mistress of the house (two or three brothers often live in one house when large, as was the case here). While we were chatting she pulled down some article to show me off a shelf, and down came a small roll of papers which scattered on the sofa, and she began collecting them carefully.

"Are you learning to write?" I asked, seeing Arabic characters in rather a disjointed way mixed with figures, as of sums, on the papers.

"Oh, no; this is a charm for the bugs," she replied. "Our house (like most old ones here) is infested, and a sheik wrote this charm for us. You see these figures?—that is because they are many; and the letters,—I cannot tell what they mean, some secret thing no doubt" (*scrib-scrab* again, probably). "We put this in a corner up there, and the creatures, he said, would all walk away."

"Have they done so?"

"Well, not yet; it is only three days yet. I fancy there are fewer, however, already."

"Do you not see that this is because the weather is become cold, and these plagues are always much less in that season? The man was tricking you, and took your money for nothing. How can you fancy that insects can read when you yourself cannot?" I continued, laughing.

She laughed heartily herself, and said, "It is really foolishness, I do think;" and agreed with me that the trouble and expense of the charm spent on white-wash, soap, and brushes, etc. would have done better.

The popular superstitions do a great deal of harm in

keeping up uncleanly habits. The religion of Mohammedans commands that they should wash when they pray, which ought to be five times a day (not that all keep to this if they are busy, and the women very rarely pray at all). This custom is of course better than nothing, and does tend to keep a certain degree of cleanliness in adult males. But superstition hinders it where specially needed, which is with young children. Moslems think it sadly unlucky to wash a baby *at all* until it is a year old. Some of the better sort have broken through this horrid custom, but as a rule it is kept to very strictly, and I believe many die from diseases brought on by dirt alone. Copts are recommended by the old women of their faith to let baptism be the first water on the child. They baptize by immersion, certainly, but no soap is in the ceremony, and it often has to last a long, long while. A dry wipe with the mother's hand, or a bit of her dress, is thought enough, and that only on the face, by too many who are by no means of the lowest class. There are exceptions, however, and the spread of education will, in time, I trust, make the exception the other way.

The writing down passages from the Koran, then washing off the writing and drinking the water, is a very favorite charm for various maladies. It seems as if man's froward heart loved to take things by contraries, for (supposing words to be ever so holy) how could *words* affect the inside of the *body?*

There are superstitious observances in other countries besides this, which seem to have come down from old Pagan times. Many of those in England came from old worshippers of Odin and Thor in the Saxon times, although the country wives who practised them had no idea of imitating Pagan ancestors, and had never heard of the false gods of those days. So in Egypt there are people who have not the least idea that they are keeping up observances which began in the worship of beasts and reptiles, etc. One of these is singular enough, and first came under my notice a few years ago. A Coptic lady sent me a message to say that her little boy was ailing. (He was more than usually precious, as the only son she had previously had had died years before; her daughter was married, and this little one was, like most late blossoms, a peculiar treasure therefore.) She wished to know if I thought it would be advisable to bring a *monkey* and keep in the house, as some neighbors suggested. The expense is considerable, she said (more than a guinea, I think), for monkeys come from a distant part of Africa, and are not found in Egypt. Still, if it would do good to the boy, she was ready to spend any thing.

"What good could he do?" I asked the teacher who brought me this message. "Is the monkey to be cooked and eaten in the form of broth by the baby, or what is it to do? He is too young to play with it."

"You don't understand,—it is the *Eye*," said the woman, mysteriously. "The monkey kept in the house is thought to *draw off* the evil influence from the child to itself."

It is needless to observe that I recommended, in preference, that if her child were really ill she should take him to the best doctor she could find, and pray for a blessing on his directions.

Now as the monkey was one of the creatures reverenced by the Egyptians, and the images of their "monkey god" are extremely numerous in collections of idols and such curiosities, and that pictures of him are to be seen on many walls in the ruined temples, etc., it seems that there is some indistinct remains of this worship left in the minds of those who even call themselves Christians, for we must recollect that the *reverence* of the heathen for false gods did not mean that they ever fancied their deities good or benevolent beings necessarily. Many, if not most, were revered with what is called "deprecatory" worship; that is, they were supposed to be persuaded or coaxed by reverence and offerings, incense and other things, and often, as we know, even human sacrifices, into letting people alone, and not doing them mischief. This is the kind of worship given by idolaters in India and elsewhere to this day; and the traces—faint perhaps, but still *traces*—of this deprecatory worship, remain here among these superstitions.

I will only relate one more,—there are hundreds, and many probably that I do not know of, but this which I am going to tell seems to me quite as clearly a remains of Pagan worship as the monkey.

Persons are said, when failing in health and spirits without any *known* cause, and sometimes when it is clearly a case of illness, but which does not as quickly yield to remedies as is expected, to be possessed by an evil spirit. The women, who seem the chief believers in this, though by no means the only ones, (indeed it may be merely as I see much more of them that they seem to me to be more full of these fancies,) declare that the only cure is to make what they call a *zikr*, a kind of dance, either sacred or magical, for they have a sort of zikr which is more of a religious observance at certain festivals. But the spirit dance is in order to drive out the bad spirit. The friends and relatives are assembled, and a grand celebration is made. I cannot speak of it from having witnessed the ceremony, as it seemed from description to be a thing no Christian ought to meddle with,—invoking of spirits, and a great deal of that sort of thing.

A young Mohammedan woman came one day to invite me to a zikr at her house, and said it would be very *amusing*.

I was surprised, and said so, asking who was supposed to be possessed.

"I am," she replied.

"But you do not look ill; what is the matter with you?"

She said she had been poorly, and no one could say why, and that she would like the excitement, and the dance, and feast, etc. And I saw that these things were *her* real motive, or at least went a great way. Still she was prepared to obey the horrible custom, which she said was to bring a sheep and kill it in the court, and as soon as a bowl had been filled with blood they would bring it to her, and she was to drink it all off at once.

"How can you do such a thing, Fatuma?" I asked.

"Oh, it is custom, I must do it, and then they will all dance round me, and clap hands, and chant; and then at last, by the middle of the night, the feast will be ready, and we shall eat and be merry, and by the next day I shall be well."

I would not go, and thought of the words of the Psalm: "Their drink-offerings of blood will I not offer, nor take up their names into my lips" (Psalm 16:4).

Letter IX
Slavery As It Is in Egypt

Egypt is full of slaves. A great deal is written and said now about the hope that the slave traffic may be stopped, but this is a much more difficult thing than people in England have generally any idea of; there are, besides the same difficulties which took so much time and trouble in the days of those good men who got the slave-trade abolished in our colonies, *other* difficulties which I need not enter on here: it is enough to say that there is no Wilberforce to labor and pray for years with his pious friends in the cause of the poor slaves, so I fear the time is not very near for their emancipation. Meanwhile, at all events, Egypt is full of them, as I said before; the cities, in particular, are teeming with negro slaves. In America (in the Southern States, that is), till the late war, and long ago in our West Indian Islands, field work was chiefly done by black slaves working in gangs, because white men could not work much in the heat of such climates. But that is not the case here; field labor is mostly done by the "children of the soil," and though a negro shepherd or herdsman is sometimes seen, the chief employment of slaves is as domestic servants. People of moderate fortune keep at least two or three; and, I am sorry to say, Christians quite as much as Moslems. Many who are in a position of life to do their own work keep a negress (who does it very imperfectly) and do nothing themselves. Of course the expense is great; really more than hiring a servant, because there is a large sum paid for the woman at first, and then she has to be fed and clothed, and being generally very wasteful, she costs a good deal. A cook or waiter in a European family will often keep a slave, and let his wife sit idly smoking a cigar all day, while this poor creature is dawdling about over the housework, and touching a broom as if it burnt her fingers. I have known of dragomen (or travelling servants) who, when on the river with English families, have actually persuaded their employers to allow them to make use of their boat to bring down a slave boy or girl whom they wanted to purchase, making the pretext that it was for the good of the said boy or girl rather than for their own convenience. Very likely the child would be kindly treated (a good many are so, no doubt, and sometimes even petted when quite young); but still, if slave traffic is a *wrong* thing, we ought not to encourage it in any way, and England, as a nation, has decided that it *is* a wrong thing.

Not long ago I was on the river for a few days' excursion, with friends, and we saw several slave-boats on their way to Cairo. One passed quite close to our boat, and we were painfully interested to watch the crowd of black faces that peered curiously at us from the cranon windows of the cabin in which they were crammed. Most were young lads of from twelve to fifteen or so; some girls seemed to be there also, but it was not easy to distinguish them. Poor things! they smiled and grinned at us, and seemed quite amused to see the white strangers looking at them, but we did not feel in at all a smiling frame of mind; it made our blood boil to think of the amount of cruelty that must have been used for this one boat-load of human beings to be dragged from their homes and penned up like cattle to be sold as if they had no souls. Surely a day of vengeance will come for these things!

But to continue my account of the negroes as they are in the towns. I do not believe that in general there is near so much bodily misery and suffering among them as there was among the American slave gangs when the planter's object was just to get as much work done as cheap and as quickly as he could, so that, if not a humane man, he fed and clothed them very coarsely, and had them beaten severely if they failed to work as steadily as he needed, and where instruction was not only hindered, but even forbidden for slaves in several of the States. Here, on the contrary, they are oftener kindly treated than not, although there is a great deal of cruelty at times, of course. I say *of course* because man is not fit to be trusted with *unlimited* power as a rule, and therefore, unhappily, it is a matter of course that when numbers have that power it will be frequently abused. One of my family once saw a neighbor of ours, when we lived in a street in Cairo, actually *stamping* upon her slave girl, whom she had first thrown down on the flat roof of the house: it was a wonder she did not kill the poor creature in her fury. But those I see are, as a rule, very well fed and dressed, often wear handsome ornaments, and appear to be treated with kindness. They are not much trusted, as the mistresses if they go out visiting for any length of time usually take the slave with them if they have only one, and if they have several leave a member of the family at home, sometimes a mere child, rather than leave the slaves with the house in their sole charge. There are a few who have proved so honest that they are trusted entirely, and beloved by the family (in which they have lived usually from early childhood) like one of its members, but these are very rare exceptions. So are the cases when slaves have been instructed, though there is no law *against* their learning, and some masters have even sent slave boys to school, if favorites, while in the establishments of the great some are taught to read even in two or three languages. But I never heard of a female being taught, because it is merely to make them useful to their masters and mistresses, and among the thousands of negress slaves here none could be found who were not in a state of utter ignorance.

A so-called Christian mistress once boasted to me that she had had her slave baptized on purchasing her, "As many of us do," she added. "O, yes; I took care of that!" "And did you teach her the meaning of the rite?" I asked. The lady burst out laughing. "Teach a thing like her! they are as cattle, those slaves!" she exclaimed. The poor woman was serving us with coffee, and heard every word. I was much pained, but knew that ignorance had as much to do with it as deliberate neglect, and that the mistress only knew the name, not the reality of Christianity. "Did you never hear the name of Jesus?" I asked the negress. "No, lady, never." "How long has she been here with you?" I said, turning to the mistress. "Ten years." "Ten years, and never heard of Jesus, and yet baptized! Why, dear friend, this is wrong. Do let me speak a little to her?"

"Willingly, but it's no use, I tell you, they are cattle."

"Yes, we are cattle," echoed the black, meekly.

"O, no, no, you are not! you have souls just as we have," I said, and went on to explain, much as I would to a child of three years, the difference between man and brutes, and the soul that was made to live in glory, and added that God wanted her to believe this, "for God *loves* you," said I.

This seemed greatly to amaze her. She had often heard God's name, usually when taken in vain, and had no distinct knowledge of Him; if any at all, it probably was that He did not care about slaves, one way or another; and when I told her of Jesus the Holy One loving us, whether white or black, and dying for our sins, the tears came into her eyes. I cannot suppose she understood all I tried to tell her, for the untaught mind is very slow to take new ideas, and I spoke as a foreigner; still something found its way into that poor soul which made the tears come forth, and she blessed and thanked me when I went away. Her mistress went to live with a married daughter afterwards, and I could not trace her. She fell into difficulties, I think, and very likely the slave was sold, for this is the first thing when money is short. But God knows all about her. We must remember to whom little is given from him will little be required. Sometimes a slave runs away from ill-treatment, and in this case, if a boy or man, he is made a soldier, or a servant to the army if not able-bodied enough for fighting: they do not like this, for they are not accustomed to exposure and hard living, and a great number of such recruits died two years ago when the army was being prepared for the war in Abyssinia.

The women now-a-days are taken by the police, and sometimes allowed to hire themselves out as servants on making declaration of ill-treatment; but a great number are taken back by their owners, who have various ways of bribing and persuading the officials.

I dare say you, who only now and then see a negro in the streets, fancy that they all look nearly alike, but in fact they belong to a great variety of tribes, and are different in feature, though in the same *style*. Some are as black as soot, or the blackest of black ink; others have a slight reddish-brown shade on the cheek-bones and forehead; some have tolerably *straight*, though flattened, noses, and large soft eyes, and a mouth only thick-lipped, but not protruding strongly. Others again (and I own they are the most numerous) seem hardly to possess a nose, properly speaking, but only nostrils, and have the whole lower half of the face and jaw-bones very forward and large, while the forehead is retreating and small; the eyes generally small in this type, and the mouth exceedingly large and coarse. I have been told that these come from Darfur, if they are large and strongly built especially. I have seen a negress who was six feet at least, and big in proportion, and when she *shouldered* her mistress's baby, the effect was droll. But a larger number have the features I have described, with a rather short figure, and a tendency to grow fat very early; when well-fed, negresses seem much disposed to stoutness in this country. Some are brought from almost unknown tribes far away in the middle of Africa, and I have seen specimens who really looked complete savages, just arrived by boat from the upper provinces (their own country being very much beyond that again). The wild, stupefied expression of face showed these poor creatures to be *below* feeling curiosity at the new things that surrounded them, as they walked after their owner, or the person who was going to sell them,—half-naked, and their black skin shining with rancid grease, and their woolly locks twisted into tight little plaits a few inches long. It is an undoubted fact that occasionally, though but rarely, a woman from a cannibal tribe has been brought up to Cairo without the knowledge of the agent or purchaser. I have heard, on good authority, of one who devoured her master's baby. The mother was very foolish to put her child into the hands of a complete savage.

The people here all *believe*, at any rate, that cannibal tribes exist in the centre of Africa, and that now and then one "turns up," although it may be very rare. In general negroes of all tribes are kind to children, and very fond of them; and if a little one is injured, it is a thousand or *ten* thousand to one that it was from the slave's ignorance and stupidity, and not from a wish to dine upon it.

But I think you will agree with me that it is a proof of the *utter* badness of the whole system of slavery, that, in spite of the *possibility* of finding a new purchase turn out a cannibal, and the *certainty* that she will be a completely wild savage, mistresses almost always prefer buying one of these newly-imported negresses to taking one who has been long in other families, though she will have learned to cook and wash, etc. This is the best answer to those who tell us it is better for them to be slaves here than to stay in their own country, "because," as a friend once said who had been persuaded by the dragoman into letting him bring down black boys to rear up as slaves, "they learn *some* good, at least." It seems, however, that they learn stealing, and a variety of other bad things; so that a raw savage is thought preferable by most employers. Can any thing be said in favor of this abominable system after this fact?

When, as sometimes happens, several ladies come to one of our meetings, or even merely as a visit, and bring slaves, I endeavor to say something special for these poor women, but those who have not been brought up in the country know Arabic very imperfectly, and cannot follow enough to get much good; others know it well, and have nearly forgotten their own tongue, indeed.

At our meeting last year (just before going for a visit to England), an elderly slave woman was so much affected by what she heard, that, while I was praying, a lady present saw the tears trickling down her wrinkled black face, and she bent eagerly forward to hear the "good words," as she said.

An instance of the love of Him who is able to save to the *uttermost* all who come to Him, through Christ, happened some years ago, when two nice little boys attended my school, and, like all our scholars, had the Bible to study. All do not profit alike, however, and as children are naturally full of play on leaving school, I was much struck with what I was told of these children reading from the New Testament to an old negress who had brought them up and was much attached to them. It seems this woman was in feeble health, and her great delight was to listen to what her young favorites read to her on their return from school, and they often spent some time by her bed thus employed instead of playing, which I think showed there was both love and religious feeling in them. When after some months the old woman became worse, and was evidently near death, some Moslem slaves, who were her friends, offered to fetch the Mollah, who is the person somewhat answering to a minister, though not exactly, and who reads from their Koran to dying persons. She refused, however; and when they urged her strongly, she replied (her master, who was of the Christian persuasion, overheard it), "No, no, I want no one but Him whom the boys tell me about; the boys' Saviour is my Saviour." And in that faith the poor slave died. Surely the Lord accepted the soul which was thus brought to touch the hem of His garment, as it were, by a little child.

It is a great mistake to suppose that slaves do more work than free persons; it is quite ridiculous to see how many of them are often kept in great houses here, and how little they do compared with what *ought* to be done, and might be *easily* done with a third of the number. I remember once counting ten women in the kitchen of a rich Coptic family; all were negress slaves, and I heard there were several more beside, men-servants; yet the kitchen was untidy and dirty, and most of them were squatting on the ground doing nothing. The stairs were imperfectly swept, and though the lady was in a splendidly-furnished room, and dressed in a beautiful muslin with diamonds and other jewels, I could not help seeing a pair of ragged old slippers and an old man's cap peeping from under a gilded sofa, orange-peel and crusts of bread in a corner, and rubbish-dust in little heaps, as if just *kicked* out of the way, instead of being cleanly swept. I do not mean that all are alike, but this was by no means an exception. They cannot have the energy which is given by the feeling that one is earning wages, and that by want of diligence one may be sent away and be without a livelihood. Treated like unreasoning creatures, they act like such, and only try to do as little and eat as much as they can, and are generally very wasteful, and the exceptions only go to prove the rule. Great numbers never live to see middle age, either from the climate of Egypt not being hot enough for those who come from a region still hotter, or else because they have less power of resisting disease than persons of lighter color; though frequently having great muscular strength, they soon fall a prey to epidemic maladies, especially such as small-pox, etc. Fresh troops of these poor people are therefore constantly being brought into the country, either stolen from their homes or seized in war, and the infamous dealers in human flesh are always in full employment, though there are no longer open slave-markets to be seen. Large under-ground places like vaults for merchandise are said to be made use of for keeping the new arrivals in till disposed of; others are sold at Khartoum, a town of importance, and the capital of

Nubia, and thence brought down and re-sold in Cairo or Alexandria. We must hope that the noble Christian men who are braving an unhealthy climate, and many dangers besides, to bring the Gospel into the negro's own country, will find a reward, and that they will rise *rapidly*, as those nations *can* who have the Bible among them. Meanwhile, the best to be done for the individuals who can be by any means *freed*, but who dwell far from their own land, is, if they are young enough to learn, to give them a good but simple education, and fit them to take an honorable place among the peasants or artisans of the land, and if girls, to be good, useful, and *respected* servants till they marry, unless any boy or girl should show capacity above the rest, so as to be fit for the position of teacher, etc. The remark made by natives here of the negroes is this: If good they are *very* good, and if bad *very* bad; and as far as my experience goes I think it is generally true. There are some slaves from Abyssinia in Egypt, but they are few compared to the negroes; the Berbers and Nubians (who are all *brown*, or coffee-colored, but not black) are very numerous in the cities; they are, however, not slaves for the most part, but free hired servants. There are a good many freed negroes, also, who have been set at liberty (or their fathers) by great men, either at their death or on some peculiar occasion, but they are rarely met with in good positions, being very idle. Besides the black races who dwell in bondage in Egypt, there are a great many *white* slaves; most of these belong to Turks residing here, though some belong to Egyptian Moslems. These are not only purchased to fill the palaces of the nobles with secondary wives (as their detestable custom permits), though this is the principal object for which the traffic is carried on, but they are also brought to act as upper servants, and often half-servant, half-companion to the great ladies. "You *hire* lady's maids in England, I believe; we *buy* ours," said a noble lady to me one day, pointing as she spoke, with a very satisfied smile, to a row of young women smartly dressed, who stood with folded arms at the end of the large room, doing nothing, but ready to bring their mistress a light for her cigar, or a glass of water, or a handkerchief, if wanted. *One* would have performed these mild duties alone with ease, but they like *show*, and the white slaves generally stand all in a row when visitors call. They at other times make clothes for their lady and themselves, dust furniture, make delicate dishes of cookery, and receive guests, folding their outer mantles, etc. But coffee is made by the black women, and all sorts of rough work also are done by them, so that the white slave has usually an easy life, and fares luxuriously every day. Still, it is the life of a canary-bird rather than of a rational being; the cage is gilt, but it *is* a cage. Some of these purchased lady's maids are given in marriage to favorites of their lady's husband, and a good-natured mistress is said to ask a slave, whom she specially approves, if she would like to be married, as in that case a match shall be found for her. Others, who have become middle-aged in one family, and have been brought up in it from childhood, prefer remaining as they are, and often act as a sort of matron to train new purchases, and to superintend the negress cooks.

I do not say these women are as a *rule* unhappy; the crying injustice of being bought like cattle does not strike them, shut up as they are, and most have been taken too young to recollect and regret the lost family; still they have generally a dull, vacant expression, unless excited by any thing, and are apt to be very selfish, as one might expect indeed. There are often quarrels and jealousies, as is generally the case when a number of women are shut up together with little to do.

And any who have been old enough to remember a home, what must it be to them? Many years ago a friend took me to see the family of a wealthy Turk resident here, whom she was acquainted with, and as we could then only speak a very little Arabic, and no Turkish, the master of the house accompanied us to his wife's apartment to interpret for us, as he spoke French. The lady was a very sweet-looking woman, and I do not think could have been unkind to her slaves, but one of them looked very unhappy; the master called our attention to her, observing that we ought to look at that girl, whom he had bought for a present to his wife recently, "because she is," said he, "so very like some of your country-women" (he had been both in France and in England, it seemed). "She is from some mountain tribe," he added, "I do not exactly know from what place, and was taken in battle." Poor girl! she turned red when pointed at, and hung down her head for a minute, and then looked up and tossed it with a haughty air; yet not really haughty, rather as if she would say, "I want to be free, and I *ought* to be free!" She seemed about fifteen, and really was extremely English-looking, with her light auburn hair, and blue eyes, and tall figure. I so often thought of her, and wished I could have helped her in any way. Probably it was only one case among many.

I cannot say much about the others,—the numbers who are in the miserable plight of being in a wife's position without her rights or privileges. I need only say that the humblest English matron who ever wore a wedding-ring need not wish to change places with such, though they are covered with gold and jewels, and waited on like a princess, which, if a favorite, is often the case. The hard-working single woman, who belongs only to God and herself, holds in reality a higher position than the richest and fairest of these white slaves, dwelling as in a cage behind the mysterious-looking curtain that hangs before the entrance to the female portion of all great houses in the East, which apartments are called "Hareem," meaning, the forbidden. This abode is guarded by black slave men, similar to those alluded to in Scripture (Daniel and Esther, and other books). No other man but the master can go into this part of the house. Royal personages and wealthy pachas have immense palaces, where two or three hundred white slaves reside, and two or three of these expensive establishments. The law of Mohammedans allows them four legal wives, but few have more than two or three, even among great men (the *poor*, but one); each wife will have several white slaves of her own, so that, altogether, the number is very considerable. These poor young women chiefly come from countries near the Caucasus Mountains,—Georgia and Circassia. The Circassians, whose name is familiar to every one from the savage conduct of the Circassian irregular troops in the late war, are a fierce, warlike people, and must have peculiar hardness about their nature, as for centuries they have (many among them, that is) had the habit of selling their little daughters to Turkish slave-dealers. I cannot learn that the other mountain tribes sell their children, unless driven to desperation in times of grievous famine; but Circassians think it as good for their children as for themselves, and deliberately part with them in this way.

"We are better off here," said a little Circassians slave to an English lady I knew. "Our mothers are very poor, and could only give us hard fare and bad clothing; here we have nice food and pretty dresses and jewels." I thought, on hearing this remark, "How little, my poor child, do you know of a mother's love!" Who that knows it would think dainty food and jewels worth more, and how hard must be the heart that sends away her little one for gold! However, I do not suppose all Circassian mothers do so; many children are doubtless stolen, as they always are from Georgia, it appears.

Both these races are celebrated for good looks; not that *all* Circassian women are beauties. I have seen a great many who had nothing except a fair skin that was particularly remarkable; but others are extremely handsome, and the type (or style of face) resembles the English more than any other. The Circassian women have in general fine hair of auburn or light brown, and gray or brown eyes, with a white skin; Georgians are generally dark-eyed, with dark brown hair, but fair complexion also. They are alike in being naturally intelligent, but are stupefied by their false and unnatural position in life, and by idleness and luxuriant habits. All are brought up as Mohammedans, of course, and learn Turkish and Arabic so early that they forget their own languages. Some few learn (if they are favorites in the family) with their little mistresses, in the palaces of great pachas, who latterly have adopted the custom of bringing a European teacher to give some instruction in French and music to their daughters; they would in such cases learn to read in Turkish from a master. But a mere outside teaching, where the heart and soul are left out, and where the instruction stops altogether at the age when we think girls are just beginning to profit by what they learn, does not change or improve the character much. It is better than nothing; but it is surprising how few seem to care to keep up the little they know. The girl I told you of, who was glad her parents had sold her because of the fine clothes and nice things she obtained, was one of those who had a little education; but being able to play a few tunes on the piano, and read tolerably in two languages, or even three, does very little good if the mind is still so uncultivated that there is no *wish* for instruction.

The being from infancy deprived of all relations, all *family* life, has a very bad effect on the disposition. We know that in the case of poor orphans in England, who are reared in schools, the want of family and home often hinders their developing in many ways as well as other young people, and that "cottage homes" for these little strays are found to answer better. But the poor little white slave children have not the wholesome discipline of a school; and the harem life, from what I know of it, is, I should think, the worst possible training. Luxurious without *comfort*, irregular though profuse in every thing, surrounded by women accustomed to look out each for herself, and with neither parents, sister, brother, aunts, or any one *belonging* to them, it is no wonder if they are generally selfish and devoted to dress, eating, and all the lower pleasures. The exceptions must have remarkably amiable dispositions, and such there are among them, as I can testify.

"I never knew what *family* love *meant* till my little boy was born, because I never had any one that belonged to me," said a sweet young woman to me one day, who is more fortunate than most white slaves in her lot, being married to a worthy man, and his sole wife, respected as well as loved. But she had evidently felt the strange loneliness of heart of being a solitary one among hundreds brought up by royalty and petted from a child, beautiful and wealthy; still the heart had yearned after something, it knew not what; and when after her little son's arrival she tasted the joy of mother's love, she then understood what it was she had been vaguely longing for. "There are," she said, "so many hundreds like me, who have never known parents, brother, or sister, or any relative at all"; and there was a look in the lovely wistful eyes, as if she would say, "There is surely something wrong somewhere; it ought not to be *so!*"

I know two white slaves who were purchased years ago by a rich merchant as wives for his two sons, and brought here from Constantinople. They reside in Cairo, and the two little girls of the two brothers have for some time come to my school, and I often visit the mothers, who are very pleasant and gentle in their manners, and so cleanly and nice in dress and habits that they are a contrast to some of their neighbors; for Turkish families, and those brought up in them, are much more cleanly than Egyptians; and it is right to give credit to every one for what they deserve.

Well, I one day asked one of my friends if she could recollect any thing about her childhood, or if she had been too young when sold, as is often the case. "Oh! I recollect very well," she said, "I was about so high," holding her hand at the height of a child of from five to seven years old. "My father had been killed in some battle, and my mother had soon followed him. I was reared by an old grandmother, from whom I used to hear this. She was partly blind, and therefore could not, I suppose, watch me carefully enough. I was at play at our door one day in the street, and a strange man came near and held out his hand with some sweetmeats, which he offered me. Childlike, I accepted them, and he then said, beckoning me on, that he had some more and prettier ones just down the street a little farther. So I went, fearing nothing; and as we turned the corner, suddenly he covered my face and flung me on a horse and galloped off, and I recollect no more,—I was so frightened. It is all dark till I see myself again in a great city, just arriving, and afterwards knew that this was Stamboul (Stamboul is the Turk's name for Constantinople, as I dare say you know). When there, I was bought by an old Turkish lady, who was kind enough, and had me taught to sew and embroider; but when I was still young she died, and her heirs sold me with her property, and my husband's father purchased me. A great many children in our countries are stolen by means of sugar-plums," she added; "it is a common trick; there are men who go about on purpose, as I have heard." She does not know whether her country is Georgia or Circassia, or some province near these regions; but her face is like the Georgian style, being fair, with dark eyes and hair.

We often see men of the Circassian race (who are Mohammedans) on their way to Mecca as pilgrims; they do not stay long in Cairo, as they go on to Suez to take ship for Arabia (Mecca being the holy city of the Mohammedans, which they visit as a religious act, if possible, at least once in their lives). During the short stay of the various pilgrims, we see many from distant lands, and, as I said, Circassians among them. Many of these men have a cast of feature and complexion strongly reminding one of Englishmen, though I think in general they are shorter in stature than is usual with well-grown Englishmen. But what a difference in countenance and expression!—such fierce, wild, cruel-looking fellows too many are, and stalk about the streets with a ferocious look, which does not make one desire their acquaintance, and generally a hand is resting on the great belt they wear, in a suspicious manner, this belt being literally *stuffed* with knives, daggers, and pistols of various kinds. And yet, when we see the complexion and features so like what we are accustomed to see at home, how strongly comes the thought, Who made us to differ? If it were not for God's grace and an open Bible, we might be blood-thirsty ruffians like them. There are, alas! bad and ruffianly men in England as elsewhere to be found; but, thank God, we are not a nation of cut-throats or child-sellers,—there is "salt" among us. But let us beware; if England ever gives up the Bible, the salt will lose its savor, and then is only fit to be trodden under foot, as the Scripture says (Matthew 5:13).

Let us pray to be kept by God's power and mercy from letting go our title-deeds to forgiveness and eternal life; and let us also pray for those who are in bondage, of whatever kind, that many among them may be gathered into the fold and made free in Christ; and let us not forget to pray that the Lord may soon come again, to receive the glory of a renewed world and reign Prince of peace, putting down the oppressor and the tyrant,—when Jerusalem as the *centre* of the earth is purified and sanctified,—when "the streets are full of boys and girls playing in the streets thereof" (Zechariah 8:5). Oh! then will be no more the cruel stealing of poor, innocent little ones. They may play safely and fear nothing; for *then* shall the "crooked be made straight and the rough places plain" (Isaiah 40:4).

Letter X
The Village

The cultivators of the ground, who, as well as keepers of cattle, are usually called Fellaheen (Fellàh, the accent on the last syllable, being the word in the singular) inhabit the villages strewn over the great plain of Egypt; a solitary hut or cottage is not to be seen; all are gathered into villages, and the "country," as we say in England, in contrast to town, is by citizens here generally spoken of as peasants', or "farmers' country."

The dress and habits are more different from those of the town than in many other places, partly because the peasants cling much more to old ways. The cultivator, even if quite wealthy, has the same style of garment as the laborers, only better in quality and more abundant; and his wife wears the same ample checked blue mantle, with its fringed border, as her poorer neighbor, only that it is good and strong, and bordered with crimson silk, and conceals a gold necklace and earrings within its folds.

The wealthy cultivator does not inhabit a mere hut such as I described in telling you of the habitations of the poor. In most of the larger villages are found from one or two to perhaps eight or ten houses of a better description, composed of two courts or yards, one within the other, with open rooms, or rather sheds, just roofed over with rough beams, or more frequently *reeds*; in one of these cattle are housed at night, in another the people carry on all the work that is not done in the open court, or if it be so windy as to make a little shelter desirable.

Shelling beans, husking maize, sifting wheat, grinding flour, which in the country is usually by a hand-mill, and all cooking, is carried on either in the yard or the sheds, which are sometimes of a considerable size, in other houses small, according to the owner's means. In all a sort of raised seat is found in one of the sheds, which is called the salamlik; this is the room where men guests are received; they are never taken into the inner rooms, which belong to the women. On this raised seat, or *ledge*, for it is nothing more than a stone or brick ledge, is spread a carpet or mat, when guests come, and there they smoke and drink coffee, and I have seen carpets of great beauty and value from Persia or Damascus brought out on these occasions, in houses of a very humble appearance, and with scarcely any furniture. The inner rooms are one, two, or three little dens, without windows, and with low doors, dark and close therefore, used for sleeping in cold weather, and for keeping any thing of value, as they have a lock. From these receptacles are brought out the carpets mentioned, which are rolled up carefully, the brass cooking utensils used on occasion of a feast, and the hard-stuffed pillows, that answer instead of chairs, being placed for the guest to lean his back or arm on, as he sits upon the carpet. In a farmer's house where I was visiting on the banks of the Nile, the good woman remarking I must be tired, having walked some way, obligingly went into her inner room and fetched a pillow or cushion of a peculiar shape, covered with the hide of a calf, with the hair on; it was extremely comfortable on a rather cold winter day; it was only stuffed with straw, and was homemade, but I thought it ingenious. Most rich farmers' wives have in this same den a good-sized box painted green, and ornamented with brass; this is sometimes called a bride's box, as every country-woman brings one to contain her clothes and little treasures when she marries, and many contain handsome sets of gold jewels, though in general these are worn constantly by the possessor, and not kept for "high days" only. I do not say I approve of women spending much on gold and jewels to put on, and it looks very much out of place to see, as one does in this country, gold coins hung round the neck when the dress is both dirty and torn. But we cannot look on it, as we should in England, as a *mere* love of finery, for the jewels are all the woman can lawfully keep if she be divorced, as the wretched law of the Moslems allows, for any thing or *nothing*, so that, but for some of these gold things, many a poor creature would go forth to starve. The Christian Egyptian cannot be treated in this way, but if left a widow, the law permits her husband's brothers, and father, if living, to take most of the property, to the exclusion of the children, at least only allowing them a small share, and the widow a still smaller. So her necklace is often her only bank; for whatever is on her person they cannot touch. I know more than formerly now about those passages in Scripture speaking of the "*cause*" of the widow and fatherless, since I have learned how such are pushed out of their little possessions in the East, and how little the law protects them.

But to return to the farmers' dwellings. The country houses, as well as huts of the poor, have still, in most cases, the old wooden lock and key, which, when I first was in Egypt, was the only one ever seen, except in European houses; the hired house in which I lived, in a native quarter, had a key a foot long I remember. Now, European keys are gradually coming into use, but the old kind, though very clumsy, have an interest in our minds, because it is evident they are the keys alluded to in the Bible, when Isaiah the prophet says, "The *key* I will lay on his shoulder" (Isaiah 22:22); it would be almost absurd to think of one of our little keys laid as a weight on a man's shoulder; but a great heavy wooden thing might be put there, as in the East every thing is carried either on the shoulder or head that can by any means be put there. The wooden key has notches to fit the corresponding ones in the lock, and are very fidgety and troublesome to open for those not long used to them.

Village dwellings near the river are generally surrounded by a palm grove, and some have two or three palms planted in their yards; not unfrequently a palm-tree is used as one of the posts of the doorway. The light shade thus given is very pleasant in the fine winter weather of Egypt. Now and then a house belonging to a great man, and occupied by his agent (or by his family now and then for a change), will be seen in a village distinguished by whitewashed walls and glass windows; though these are generally very primitive inside, and built only of mud brick. A curious addition to most villages is the Egyptian pigeon-house, which is quite original. It consists of a great number of rude earthen pots, built into a mud wall, in the form of a *dome*, or little tower; in this the birds make their nests, and it is very singular to watch them all coming out of their jars in a flock, and flying off to seek food, and again returning at night, and each knowing its own place. "They shall fly as doves to their windows," probably alluded to some such kind of pigeon-house (Isaiah 60:8).

I have already told you about the huts of the poor people, who of course are the most numerous, and which resemble those in the suburbs of towns and inside the towns also, in some quarters. Many small hamlets consist of nothing but a cluster of such miserable huts as those, but in the larger villages there will be usually found some people who are well off. A large tree is very often found near the middle of a village, where the men assemble to chat of an evening, as is the case in European villages. The favorite tree is either a sycamore-fig, or a mulberry, both of which grow to immense size.

The countryman has plenty to do during the chief part of the year, and gets through a great deal on very frugal fare. If taxed only in moderation, and not allowed to be *fleeced* by under officials, acting like the "publicans" or tax-gatherers in our Lord's time in Judea, who robbed the people to fill their own purses, the peasant would have enough for his simple wants, and none need suffer, because the land is so fertile, and brings either two or three successive crops in a year. Ploughing is done by oxen or buffaloes, as is the threshing or treading out of the corn. For this business a man sits in a sort of wooden chair without legs, and with some simple machinery under it, which crushes the corn as the oxen draw it about on a space of hard beaten earth; the feet of the animals and the machine together knock out the grains. *Winnowing* is done with a shovel, tossing up the corn on a breezy day. They leave the grain out in heaps till it is sold, the climate being so dry.

The cattle form a great part of the peasant's wealth, and are of various kinds. The Egyptian cow is large, and capable of working, and both cows and oxen are used in the water-works, etc. But buffaloes are more numerous, being cheaper to keep and very strong, besides giving a greater quantity of milk, though the butter is not equal to cow's butter, nor will it keep fresh so long. The Egyptian buffalo is larger than the cow, and is rather an unwieldy creature to look at, of a dark-gray color, with scanty rough hair on the skin, and huge horns, and projecting bones on its back; but it is generally of a very gentle disposition, and is frequently ridden by the children of its owner when going to and from pasture, and a buffalo calf is constantly to be seen at the door of a hut with the baby playing beside it. In the lower lands the buffalo does particularly well, as it delights in water, and is seen in the time of inundation swimming across the canals or the river (often with a man on its back), or wading in pools up to its great horns, giving occasional puffs of satisfaction at the bath. A great many goats are also kept. There are two or three varieties, but the commonest is a kind with rather short hair, usually brown or chestnut, marked with white, and many of which are hornless, the he-goats almost always so. A long-haired goat is not uncommon, however, black or white. Sheep are very often brown, or white with a black neck and head. Great flocks of goats and sheep are to be seen on the banks of the river or by the canals; in warm weather they come from a distance to drink, the pools being then dry, and it is very pretty to see them resting in the shade of a tree in the heat of the day, and recalls the words of Scripture in the Song of Solomon,—"Tell me, O thou whom my soul loveth, where thou feedest, where thou makest thy flock to rest at noon" (Song of Solomon 1:7).

The arable land is not in Egypt divided by hedges, as in England; measurement is the only thing to decide the limits of the different fields, though of course trees, canals, etc. serve as landmarks to the eye. The measurement is made by a reed of a certain length, and in writing of deeds and leases it is always said so many "reed lengths." I was struck years ago by first seeing a man measuring ground in this way; he had a long smooth reed of the kind before described in his hand, and laid it down and lifted it up, making a running leap with great dexterity, and thus went on springing from measure to measure quickly, yet as it seemed accurately. Another man accompanied him, walking behind,—at a much slower pace, however. Perhaps you may recollect, in the measuring of Ezekiel's temple (in the fortieth chapter of Ezekiel), the reed of six cubits long and the height and breadth of different parts being said to be "one reed." So this is one among the many things that remain unchanged from the old days. A yet more interesting reference is to that verse in Revelation where John says the angel that talked with him "had a golden reed to measure the city, and the gates thereof, and the wall thereof" (Revelation 21:15).

Those villages which are near the desert have usually a fence of these same reeds upon the side exposed to the high winds and drifting sand of the desert, which would injure the crops. Some Bedouin families, descendants of the wandering Arab tribes who had land given them to induce them to settle, by Government, a good many years ago, make huts of reeds, sometimes a sort of square "wigwam," sometimes a mere enclosure, without any roof, and in these poor abodes they actually live, except for a short time in winter, when they sleep in the little round mud hovels with a hole for a door, of which a few added to the reed dwellings make up their little hamlet, with occasionally a tent of ragged goat's hair, though these last more properly belong to the wandering Bedouins. I have often visited colonies of this kind; one visit which had much interest connected with it was in the winter of 1877. The Nile overflow had been very low that autumn, and much distress was the consequence, especially on some of the districts depending only on the river-flow for watering. This was the case with the poor little colony of Bedouins. Their land was usually just sufficient to provide corn for their bread, and fodder for their few goats and camels, but not a single ear of wheat would grow for want of the water, and they had only existed by selling from time to time a goat or a camel, and living on the corn bought with its price as long as they could. As to clothes, all they had were in rags, and several of the children had none at all. The reed enclosures, with three or four tiny round mud huts, were all their habitations,—five or six families I think there were. We bought some eggs of the poor women, and paid a little extra to help them,—the more willingly that they did not clamor for money as so many do in the villages where Europeans are often seen. I do not think these poor Bedouins had ever seen a visitor in their miserable little abode before; they were greatly surprised evidently, but very civilly asked us, not to "come in" exactly,—for unless we crawled on hands and knees we *could* not have done so,—but to sit down in their enclosure of reeds, which kept off a little of the high wind and the clouds of dust which it brought, and one kindly offered her husband's goat's-hair cloak as a seat; but it was not inviting, and with many thanks I said I preferred the sand. The men of the company were going to join some companions in an expedition for selling one of their remaining goats, and some of our party had gone on to a much larger village a little way off, so that I was left alone with the women, about six of whom, with a few children, sat in a circle round me, and after a little talk, in order to introduce the subject and make friends with them, I asked if they would listen while I read something out of God's word. "You know how to read, then?" asked an old woman; "but your book is, I suppose, in Frank language?" (meaning some European tongue). "No, it is Arabic." "Well, that is wonderful," said she; "read and let us hear." I was in my turn surprised to find so much intelligence and intellect in women whose outward appearance was so low and wretched. The little that peeped above their face-veils showed thin, sunburnt, wrinkled faces, worn by hardship, and with ugly features, yet many a smooth-skinned and jewelled lady to whom I had vainly offered the Gospel might have taken a lesson from their earnest attention. They were scantily clad, and ragged, as I said before, their *wiry* brown arms and legs showing through many a rent; but God looks not at the outside, but the heart, and one of these in particular seemed to me as if a ray of light was gradually finding its way into her soul, as her little twinkling eyes sparkled with inward pleasure as I read of God's love to sinners, and explained that beautiful text, "Knock, and it shall be opened to you," etc. (Matthew 7:7). "Now suppose you went just as you are to a pacha's palace and knocked," said I, "what answer would you get?" "Why, they would drive me off, and most likely beat me," replied the old woman. Then I showed her how *God* is different from man, and explained that knocking and seeking, etc. meant praying, and afterwards taught her and another, who was also very attentive, the short and precious prayer, "God be merciful to me a sinner." They repeated it over and over after me, and I tried to give them some idea of Christ dying in our place, and how that *is* God's love to man. The hour was a very interesting one that I spent among these poor women. May God grant that some seed may take root in their hearts, and be like bread cast on the waters, to be found after many days!

This has led us away somewhat from the actual Egyptian peasant's life (for the Bedouin Arab, whether the wandering tribes of the desert, or these poor half-starved colonists, are all of Asiatic origin, and not properly Egyptians), but being *inhabitants*, and with the same language as the people of the soil, it seemed that a little notice of them might not be amiss. Besides, the mention of *reeds* naturally brought the reed huts and the poor dwellers in them to mind.

The men of the colony had gone, I told you, to sell a goat, and this brings us to the village markets, for it was to a market held in one of the neighboring villages that they took it, to bring back corn in exchange. These markets are held weekly in certain villages, on certain days, much as with us; but the articles sold are in some respects as different as the look of the sellers and buyers. Very early in the morning the countrymen may be seen on the high causeway, along the river-side, or canal, driving cattle, or donkeys, or camels laden with produce of the fields, according to the season;—in winter the beautiful green clover; in early spring the same, with its white flowers; in summer, chopped straw, in huge panniers of netting slung over camels' backs, or in boats piled up with the same, if on the river-side. These men are generally fine and sturdy looking; their swarthy complexions, which do not suit European dress, look very well in their own white turbans, with great mantles of either white or brown, or of a dark blackish-purple color, hanging over their shoulders, and their feet bare. Sometimes you see a man carrying a pair of nice red or yellow leather shoes over his shoulder by a string, to put on when he is in the market with his friends, but he walks better barefoot when he has some distance to come.

While he is busy with the sheep and goats, the corn and maize and red lentils, the fodder and the calves, etc., his wife and daughters have joined the crowd of countrywomen who are chattering, as women are apt to do at market in any country. They have put on their best clothes, if not too poor, as are very many, to possess any but the ragged blue garment and veil they wear. Those who *can*, however, appear in flowing veils of thin black muslin, or sometimes, though not so often, in light blue, with dark purple or blue dress, hanging loose without belt or sash, and with long wide sleeves, which, thrown back, display the massive silver bracelets, and the necklace of gold coins, or curious gold ornaments shaped like little fish (often very old, having come down from mother to daughter), or gold and coral beads. Some have, instead, a circle of plain bright silver, as thick as a woman's little finger, round the neck. Some wear—what is never seen in the city, unless on a countrywoman passing by—a nose ring. In some villages they are very much worn; in others, only here and there a woman will wear one. This ornament, which to our taste is not becoming, and must be exceedingly inconvenient, one would suppose, is of great antiquity, and appears formerly to have been worn in Palestine, though now not often met with there.

The dark blue of the dress is from the durableness of the indigo dye, which makes it more suitable for those who work in the fields than the gay prints worn in the cities. Many of the peasant women still wear strong native linen, instead of cotton, dyed of a purplish or deep blue color; and most, who can afford it, have a long crimson silk cord, with large tassels, fastened to the plaits of their hair, hanging down behind; it does not seem of any use, but they like it, and I must say it is both prettier to look at, and much more cleanly, than the detestable bunches of false hair which many young women wore not so long ago, or than a good many articles of tawdry vulgar finery on which money is wasted among us.

Almost every woman comes into market with a load on her head of some kind,—either a pitcher of sour milk, or a *skin* of the same, with lumps of butter in it, or a basket of eggs or fowls, cheese or dates, leeks or onions, or any vegetables in season. There is little except provisions of a common kind, cattle, etc., and a few colored prints, and pieces of unbleached calico, thread, etc., sold in the market; scarcely any thing of show or luxury, unless it be a few tiny looking-glasses, and clumsy combs, and red handkerchiefs in a corner. It is only of late years that a few plates and dishes are occasionally found in the houses of the wealthier farmers, the coarse red pottery of the country, made in a sort of pan, being the only earthen vessels in most village dwellings, and even those not numerous.

I recollect being once offered some bread and milk in a pan of this kind by a friendly peasant woman, who was quite hurt that I should not eat with her (when paying a rather early visit). It was on the banks of the Nile, in a large village. She was very well off for cows and goats, etc., but had not such a thing as a cup or bowl in her house, nor pan of moderate size, only the huge one which the family sat round and ate from together at supper, I suppose. I picked out a morsel or two to gratify her, but thought it an odd way of taking bread and milk, with neither spoon nor cup.

I used to wonder in those early days how they drank, till I saw them lift a pitcher of considerable weight (though much smaller than that carried on the head to *bring* water) and *pour* the draught from a height into their throats. I tried to do the same, but early habit being wanting, I only succeeded in watering my clothes plentifully, without getting more than a drop or two in the right direction.

The countrywomen are by no means as carefully veiled as the towns-people, and a great many of the poorer ones have no face-covering at all; but if they have to speak to a man, most will draw the muslin veil across the mouth and nose, holding it with one hand, or in the teeth, if both hands are busy weighing cheese or dates. Those who are in what they think proper full dress have the black face-veil I described before, but you see very few of these in the villages. They are freer in their ways, and less afraid of mixing with men in the way of business than towns-people; but still keep much more distant than is thought necessary in European countries.

Though Egyptians are naturally good-natured, and very hospitable, it is impossible for any stranger to get a lodging in a village,[1] because the habits of the people do not allow the women of the family to see or admit any one. If a friend comes to see a villager, he is received in the room I described as the salamlik, if in a rich peasant's house; if not, under a tree, where a carpet or mat is spread. A *lady* can, however, gain an entrance much more easily, of course, and though in *some* villages (either from the bigoted character of the people, or from their *sheik*, or head man, being of a superstitious nature, and disliking Christians), it would be very difficult to get on friendly terms, yet these I have found to be few compared with those in which I was received with friendly and cordial kindness.

Many years ago I was with a little party on the river in a Nile boat, and we were delayed by bad winds. Being short of bread, we landed at a small village, and tried to purchase some of the very *un-tempting* flaps of dark native sour bread, for hunger is glad of even the humblest fare. But not one would sell a single loaf. "We bake for ourselves," one sulky old woman said, "and have none for strangers." "But we will pay you well; see, here is money," said one of

[1] Unless in a sheik's house occasionally, as that may possibly contain several rooms.

the gentlemen, shaking a purse; and knowing that money is very scarce in these places, we expected success. But no, the feeling evidently was that there was some ill-luck in letting Christians get their bread. "We have none; we don't sell," was the only reply, and we returned to our boat, and had to defer our breakfast till late in the afternoon, when we reached Cairo.

Very different was the reception we found in another village (several years afterwards), when visiting on the banks of the Nile, and happened to find the good woman of a house at which we called engaged in baking. We were quite unknown to her, but she politely asked me and the lady who accompanied me to come in and rest, while the gentleman of the party had to go with the master of the house, a respectable countryman, to the outer court, where the men's seat was prepared for him by spreading a carpet. We apologized for coming in where the women were so busy, but said we should like to see how they did it, if not troublesome. The woman begged us to stay "all day," as she said, and entreated us to eat as much of her hot bread as we liked. We were not in want of any, but tasted it to please her, with thanks for her civility. You would have been amused to see the process. This was dourra, or maize bread, which is often used when the store of wheat is finished. It is more troublesome to make by far, because the maize flour has scarcely any *gluten* in it, that is, it will not *stick* together, as the children say, without great difficulty and being much worked. In America, I believe, they mix a portion of common flour with it, and thus make pretty good bread, but here they were using it because they had no other flour; so the plan was to let it *rise* with leaven (or sour dough) very high indeed, till an extremely light moist sponge; the vessel this woman had was as big as a washing tub, and was brimming over with the dough, which was too sour for our taste, but they relish it so. One woman took up a small piece and threw lightly on a well-floured wooden shovel or spade, with a short handle, and then cleverly shook it till the soft dough became a very thin flat cake; she then quickly shoved it on to another spade, held by the baker, who was squatting at the oven door, and who popped it into the heated place, and pulled out the cake within, handing it to a third, who laid it on a heap of large thin pancake-like loaves beside her. Their rapid action was very amusing to watch; I never saw any thing done more nimbly and handily, but with all their quickness it was a long process. They said maize would not do in any other way; as they chiefly lived on bread, and there were several growing lads in the family, this huge quantity would only last three or four days, the mother told me!

The village houses never have any sort of garden around them; if a farmer has a garden at all, it is a patch of vegetables at some little distance, under the palm grove, or adjoining his cornfield or other crops. There are beautiful gardens belonging to the great men in some parts of the country, but the poor people have not yet learned to see that when they live near the water, (for otherwise certainly the expense would make it impossible for a poor man,) a few flowers and pot-herbs cost nothing but a little trouble. It is merely ignorance, for they all like flowers, especially sweet-scented ones, and if water, as I said, is near, plants will grow very rapidly in such a climate. I hope in time they may learn to improve their dwellings, both within and without, and not to mind a little trouble for the sake of a great deal of comfort, and some innocent pleasure.

Letter XI
Town Life

The Egyptians are naturally ingenious in handicraft, but formerly seem to have carried their manufactures to greater perfection, especially considering the want of implements in old times. In some respects they have lost undoubtedly; the beautiful wood-carving, for which they were so famous, is lost as an art; no one living can do it now in the old style. Formerly, wooden lattices, carved in a variety of patterns, and most ingeniously, were used instead of glass windows, which are of course more convenient in some respects, but, on account of the glare of the sun, wooden blinds of some sort are quite necessary, and the old carvings are very imperfectly supplied by modern Turkish blinds or Italian shutters. The fine linen of Egypt, so famous of old, has now disappeared, and only a coarse kind, worn by peasants, is made, good in its way, but by no means choice; the hand-looms cannot compete with the steam of Europe, and both cotton and linen from Europe are procured more cheaply than they can make them. The coarse kind I allude to keeps its steady sale up, however, because the peasant women prefer what is *lasting*, and it wears three times as long as any of our manufactured goods of a similar style. They also weave some silk for the same reason; those who want a good quality that will wear long prefer the native kind to the cheaper fabrics of France. Their silk is dear, but very lasting, and of a beautiful pattern; the native ladies hardly ever use it now, but the tradesmen, merchants, and wealthier artisans use it for their *kaftans* and waistcoats.

Though the old custom of selling every kind of article, as well as making them, in special quarters, each for itself, is a good deal broken in upon by the introduction of European shops for mixed goods, still it keeps up for all *native goods,* and is the general custom of the cities in Egypt, as in most if not all Eastern cities. These quarters, composed of one, two, or three streets, as may be, are called "sooks," translated *market*, but they do not answer at all to our market; they use the word more widely in fact. My servant will tell me, "The market for vegetables is over," just as one in England might say; but he will add, "Shall I go to the brass market for those pans?" or "to the shoe market for the red shoes for the schoolgirls?" Europeans often call them bazaars, and natives, also, indeed understand the word, but it is, I believe, an Indian one, meaning the same as "sook," merely a place where goods are displayed. English ladies now give the name to a fancy sale for charitable purposes, but the original signification was widely different. There are in Cairo two or three *shoe* quarters, consisting of narrow streets lined with small den-like shops, occupying the ground-floor of large houses (used as dwelling-houses). In these dens, amidst dozens of red and yellow native shoes of various kinds, the owner, with sometimes an assistant, sits cross-legged stitching away, and receiving his occasional customers. They are *but* occasional, except at the festival times, and then a great business is done. Every artisan in town, and every peasant in the village for miles round, comes to buy a new pair of shoes "for the feast," and every boy and girl above the position of a beggar expects this treat, though they may often go barefoot, when this pair is worn out, till the feast comes round again. Being much cheaper than European shoes, the man must be poor indeed who cannot afford his children at least the commonest kind. They are hard bargainers, however, and as the system of fixed price does not yet prevail, a good deal of time is often spent over a small thing.

"By your eyes it is too dear," says a sturdy, bronze-faced countryman, balancing on his labor-hardened hand a pretty little pair of red pointed shoes, suited to the small delicate feet of a little Egyptian of some two or three years.

"Dear! on the contrary, they are too cheap; only it is for the feast, I should otherwise ask more," replies the turbaned shoemaker, pulling his thread out of a great pair of stout yellow slippers with very thick soles (meant for peasant's wear).

"Six piastres for these little things, and not strong either! I will give three and a half."

"May God open" (answering to "God forbid I should do so"), replies the man of shoes, taking the pair out of the other's hand, and hanging it on a hook before him.

"As I promised my little Ayusha, and they are just her size," says the poor man, looking tenderly at them, and speaking half to himself, half to the tradesman, "come, say four, and I will have them."

"By the Prophet, it is not possible,—no, it is finished; four indeed!"

The peasant jerks his mantle over his shoulder, and turns away; then looks back and says, "Four and a half,—I am going away."

"Well, I am giving them away, but for your sake,—there!" and the bargain is concluded.

I give the conversation as I heard it last winter; I was buying something near, and could not help listening, and the man, with the true Egyptian love of sympathy, turned to me to exhibit them. I hope Ayusha was pleased.

The saddlers' quarter is at least as important as the shoemakers', donkey-saddles in particular being an article of constant use here. Formerly, when only two or three carriages were to be found in all Cairo, every one rode everywhere on donkeys. They answered completely to cabs, etc., and had the advantage of being very cheap, and of being able to go into narrow streets impassable for carriages. Now many of these narrow streets have been widened, and many more carriages are used; still the donkey is a very useful helper for the town, and in the country is the usual mode of conveyance along the narrow cross-roads.

The native saddle is made of red leather with a curious *hump*, stuffed with straw, in front, and the bridles and head-fittings are adorned with tassels of colored cotton, wool, or even silk, so that they are very gay affairs when new. The horse furniture and saddle are still more so; they are covered with cloth or velvet, and have (when made for great men) a beautiful fringe of gold or silver, and cases for pistols at the side.

Then we have the sugar market, where not only sugar, but dried fruit and other groceries are sold; the scent market, in a quarter so narrow that scarcely even a single donkey can pass, and where the air is heavy with the rich odor of frankincense and myrrh, and various Arabian scents much prized in the harems; and the gold and silver market, where the native bracelets and necklaces are made, and where also gold thread and wire and silver spangles, etc. for embroidery are sold, by weight. Silk for this purpose is found in a quarter close by, and you would be amused to see the seller winding the fine silk on his bare foot, holding it with the toe, while he dexterously winds the needed quantity, and then weighs it in his pretty little brass scales. From these delicate articles we come to much coarser ones,—the makers of wooden combs, wooden pegs, etc.; then to the workers in palm frames for cages, hampers, and a great many other things; then the street of the sieve-makers, where every family sifts its own flour for bread: sieves are a very important household article. Then we have the brass quarter, where the quantities of brazen vessels in use, and for which Cairo is famous,—from the immense pan used by washerwomen, and the caldron which would easily boil a lamb whole if needed, down to the pretty little brass coffee-pot used by the shopman for his single cup of coffee. The *din* in this quarter is deafening, and I am sure all who live near it must early lose their hearing.

It would be too tedious to go through all the various trades; but I must mention one more which is peculiar to Egypt, and used to puzzle me when a stranger here. A whole street was occupied by men, each in his den, with a very simple machine, which assisted him in twisting long ropes of crimson silk and large tassels of the same, with a little black and white sometimes worked up with it. At last I found these were merely an ornament, but an indispensable one in their eyes, for the countrywomen, as before described. When muffled in their mantles, of course it is hidden. I supposed the good woman is happy in knowing it *is* there, even if little displayed; and we must allow that in civilized Europe women *will* persist in wearing articles quite as useless and *much* more troublesome,—such as chignons, trains, high-heeled shoes, and others.

A great many tobacco shops are found scattered through the town, not in a special quarter, the people being much given to smoke. As a rule, their tobacco is *less* unwholesome than that used in Europe by far, being milder in quality. The peasants do not go about smoking all day, as in Germany and many other countries; they only take a smoke while resting, usually from a long cherry-stick pipe, handed from one to the other, or a water-pipe made of a cocoanut (of which numbers are brought from India) and a *reed*; the smoke is passed through the water by this means, and elderly men especially seem to enjoy this luxury. The wealthy have the same thing, but made of glass, and with a colored tube of great length, that winds round the bowl. Paper cigars are also in great use, and are now seen more frequently than the long pipe, or chibouk, as it was called, which older ladies still however prefer. In the harems the ladies smoke a great deal, and I think it injures their health. Even women of a humbler class often smoke cigars a great deal, but you seldom see countrywomen smoke, and they are the healthiest of the population. I cannot make out that these inveterate smokers are ever the better for it, and certainly they waste both money and time; but this last is not yet valued as it ought to be here.

Formerly each district of the city had an arched doorway to the chief of the narrow little streets of the quarter, and a huge massive wooden door, which was locked after a certain hour at night; and if by a rare chance I had been to see friends, and was returning after ten o'clock, my servant had to arouse the door-keeper, who was asleep on a bench beside this great door, and get him to unlock it; often a quarter of an hour was spent in waking him up and waiting by persons who returned late.

Many of these doors are now taken away in the making of the new streets, and the largest thoroughfares in the city (though only these) are lighted now with gas. Formerly we had to take a lamp if going out even the shortest distance after sunset; but even now it is needful if going to a wedding, for instance, or any visit to a native family out of the broad highway.

The little old-fashioned lamps were of prepared paper or calico, made to fold up flat and go in a man's pocket, a piece of wax taper being carried with them. These are still found, but glass lanterns are more common with persons of the better sort, who generally make a servant (or slave-boy if they are natives) walk in front carrying it. In the narrow lanes of a great part of the city, where rubbish is always found, and where the half-wild dogs are crouching about among the dust-heaps, and stones encumber the path, it is necessary to pick the way very carefully if walking at night, and the lamp is usually held as *low* as possible, in order to throw light on the path for a few steps before the person walking. This is no doubt an old custom. Formerly, when no gas was found in Egypt, I used to watch from my window in the city passengers returning home in the short winter evenings, and each one carrying his lantern, or his servant, if a rich man, holding it before his feet, and think of the comparison in the Psalm, "Thy word is a light unto my *feet* and a lantern to my *path*" (Psalm 119:105). Just light for the way, step by step, is all we are to expect as the little lantern throws its ray on the rough footpath!

I will try to give you a glance, as it were, at some little daily scenes of city life before ending this letter, and the simplest way will be just to note down the things as they passed before me in a morning ride through part of the town at an early hour in summer. The chief difference in *winter* would be that the hour would be ten instead of seven, and that the articles brought from the country, vegetables and fruit, would be different, and the passers-by more muffled up, and the old folks sitting in sunny corners of their dusty lanes instead of choosing the shade of the old crumbling walls as in hot weather. But life in Egypt is always out-door life, at every season of the year; it is only a storm of wind, or the dust winds occasionally blowing, or the far rarer shower of rain, that sends the people in-doors. And I suppose this is the proper life for health, as the children in the grand harems, where they are rarely out of doors, are generally pale and feeble, while those who live out, especially the country ones, are generally active and strong; in spite of rags and dirt they have the advantage of those who have hardly any fresh air and sunshine.

My house is just outside the city wall, and the larger one I built for the school is only divided by the playground and my garden. As I passed through the gate, a number of the earlier scholars (boys) were already arrived, and some were playing, some looking over their lessons, others buying pieces of sweetmeat to eat with their bread for breakfast, the seller of these sticky dainties, with his stand, being just within the door, and very busy driving bargains with little fellows, who wanted as much as possible for their small coin. Many arrive as soon as the gate is opened, which is soon after sunrise, and spend a pleasant couple of hours in the shade of a nice mulberry-tree, and two or three others, planted on purpose for them in the playground. Leaving this happy group I ride down an open and wide road, with a few good houses, chiefly belonging to Syrian and Jewish families, but with a good deal of waste land waiting to be built on, and occupied for the time by a few little sheds for small traders in red handkerchiefs, common eatables, cigars, etc. A man is pruning the trees which shade this road, and ragged boys and girls are eagerly seizing the boughs and leaves as they fall, and carrying them off as fodder for their parents' goats, several of which are already enjoying the treat, their pretty spotted kids frisking about them. The donkey's head is now turning. We must leave the broad way and enter a narrow lane for a short cut into the city. In a moment we are in a purely native quarter,—mud-brick huts, or half-ruined houses, occupied by the poor, a few middle-class dwellings mingled with them; a negress, with a yellow handkerchief on her head, peeps out from one of these; a mistress in very slight garments, evidently not of the active housewife style, and but half awake, from another; but with the chief part of the inhabitants of this quarter all their life is out of doors. There sits a woman winding thread under the shade of a tree planted in her neighbor's yard. She has a pretty little twirligig of a machine, simply but cleverly made of the ever useful *reed*: she is winding for the weavers; her children are playing in the dust-heaps near her. A little farther a girl is driving her father's goats into their stable, and a whole row of blue-robed old cronies are squatted at the edge of the narrow path (road it can hardly be called) doing nothing but enjoy the air and gossip. Not a man is to be seen; they are all away at work, except a stray Jew peddler, who stops to try and coax the women to buy some of his flimsy gay calicoes, and one or two peasants with vegetables from the country, and laden asses, hurrying along to the markets. Another lane out of this has rather higher pretensions: here are shops, though of a very humble kind; the "Attar," or seller of drugs and spices, sitting in his den, a thin red-covered book in one hand and a string of beads in the other, for it is yet early for business, and he is making his devotions while at leisure, reading extracts from the Koran and reciting prayers; it is conscientious as far as it goes, certainly, and the poor man knows no better, but he is probably extremely self-righteous, as Moslem devotees always are (nor they alone indeed). Beside him is a dealer in cheap, common haberdashery, chiefly from Europe. Then a melon-seller, busy purchasing his stock from a countryman; then a Greek, who sells red earthen pans, which adorn his door in numbers; and various eatables, as dry fish, oil, etc., within.

Now we leave all these and turn down a very short, but *very* narrow lane, with some rather curious-looking, but large, houses on each side, and scarcely any windows. They are the old style, and all the windows open on the inner court, as if they turned their backs to the street; it is so narrow here that I have to squeeze close to the wall to let a great camel pass; a young lad sits on his hump merrily playing on a reed pipe as he rides slowly along; if the tune is monotonous it is not disagreeable, and it is pleasant to see him cheerful. A little girl, with a pan of some curious mess, in which oil has a share, on her head, passes next, and so close that I hold my skirt for fear of a drop of the mixture reaching it; then a dust-man, with his basket of rubbish on his shoulder, and his musical cry (strangely enough some of the least pleasant of the street callings are often announced by very good voices), and a half tune, which sounds really pretty. We reach the opening in safety, and get into sunshine and space again. The tailor who sits at the corner on his board does not seem to find the quarters as unpleasant as we should; like nearly every one he is out of doors, board and all, and a beautiful cat and kitten seated on it, for company, beside him. (In general, cats are both liked and kindly treated in Egypt.)

We now enter a wide thoroughfare, called the "new street," several nests of old huts and ruined houses having some years ago been pulled down to make it. Here we see carriages, some with Europeans, others with natives of the land, driving by; asses in plenty, from the rough-coated country donkey, with his load of bright red tomatoes, or black egg-plants from the country, to the sleek white ass of the true Mecca breed, with that equally sleek-looking merchant on his back, clad in a beautiful dark-purple gibbeh, or long robe, displaying a spotless white kaftan in front, and a goodly turban, which protects him well from the sun. Here are shabby-looking European shops (the smallest Eastern shop, poor as it may be, never has a shabby look, as the second and third-rate Europeans have), with slatternly women, and unwashed shop-boys, sweeping out their shops or drinking their coffee at the door; then we come to an open space, where several streets branch off, a plot of garden being in the centre, and great houses of the wealthy, hotels, and public buildings appear. On one side is the public garden, once a swamp, then reclaimed by the famous Mohammed Alee, and planted with fine trees, and hedges of rose and myrtle; it was a somewhat damp and unhealthy, though very pretty *wild* garden, half-way between a garden and a wilderness, in fact. Then it was let to French and Greek coffee-house keepers, and became for a few years a den of thieves, and almost impassable; finally, they have made it, as nearly as they could, into a French public garden, well guarded and kept, and planted in too formal or *trim* a style to suit the country exactly; but it will, as the trees grow larger, and the gardeners get off their guard a little, be sufficiently luxuriant by and by, no doubt!

But busy people in the morning have nothing to do with the Ezbekeeh, as this park is called; they are hastening to the various markets, either to buy or to sell, and the clerks to their offices. We pass the entrance to what is called the European market, and go through the numerous shops of modern luxuries, and European garments (of which the greater part are kept by Jews, though also some by various nationalities), and enter a quarter chiefly inhabited by Syrian silk-merchants, whose goods make a beautiful display, with their delicate colors and rare embroidery.

Then, after passing a noisy row of copper and brass makers, we reach the great cotton market, where, besides a good many really native articles, such as peasants, etc. use, there is an abundant display of Manchester cottons and prints, the latter such as you might live years in Manchester and never see, unless you visited the warerooms of a manufacturer who had dealings with Egypt. For every country has its tastes, and the canary color, which is a special favorite here for girls, and suits their jet-black hair and eyes, would not suit flaxen-headed English lasses at all; nor the orange and white stripe, which is another favorite, besides a variety of singular patterns, such as black stags galloping on a pink ground, or green herons stalking over an imaginary river of buff muslin, etc.

These little details are not for gentlemen, you know, but some of my old friends (and *all* little girls), I feel sure, like to hear about dress patterns and such humble matters, and I want to entertain them by telling what I *see*, great or little. We can leave the prints and the bead necklaces, and all the finery, now, for here is a little narrow, *very* narrow lane, only just room for one donkey, (if I meet another, one must get down and back out!) and we are now in a very different quarter: paper, ink, pens; those large bundles of dark glossy reeds hanging from the top of the little den are reed pens, the only kind with which the Arabic language can be properly written; and those little slabs of wood, painted white or red, are for children to learn upon, the alphabet being written on it by the master. They are very pretty, but get soiled so soon by dirty little fingers that we prefer cards, or better still, my great favorite, the blackboard and white chalk, used much in my school.

Opposite the paper and ink stores is the scent market, which tells its own tale; the passion for sweet scents is so strong here, that they will sometimes burn a piece of fragrant incense, and pass a tumbler over the smoke, and then fill with sugar and water, and this sherbet is thought delicious: I cannot say I enjoy *drinking* incense, though the smell is pleasant. There are scents here from Arabia which are never met with in England, and some also the name of which has an interest for us, such as the frankincense and myrrh, prized now as they were the day when they were part of the offerings brought to the infant Saviour by the wise men.

But we must leave the scent market, with its sweet odors, and the bustling cotton marts, and hasten back before the summer sun has become too powerful. These few little observations do not go very far, indeed, to show you the city and its inhabitants, but may give some idea, at least. And what is said about Cairo applies more or less to all the cities of Egypt, only those that are seaports have more Europeans, and are less characteristic than Cairo; while the smaller towns and villages again are, of course, more simply, thoroughly national in their ways than any of the great cities.

And what about the "great mixed multitude" of foreigners? I said in a former letter I would tell you a little about them; it can be, however, only a very little, for, living and working among the "children of the soil," I do not know nearly so much about the strangers. For the most part, I am sorry to say, there can be no doubt that they do more harm than good. I am not, of course, speaking of the small number of respectable Europeans who are residents for business in the great cities, and who, for the most part, only spend some years here and have no intention of residing always in Egypt. I mean by the mixed multitude the people settled here, some of them born in Egypt, others come over recently, and consisting chiefly of Greeks, French, Italians, Germans, and Maltese. Some are respectable and wealthy persons, and they have all their own places of worship, and their Consuls to manage their affairs; but a great many are not respectable, and only settled here because they could not get on at home in their country, and not a few, I fear, who *dared* not return, because they have not a good character where they came from. These set a sad example to natives of Egypt; drinking, and all sorts of bad ways, are common among them, and, alas! have been learned by those who knew little that was good, yet (especially as regards strong drink) did not know these things. Theatres were first brought here by French and Italians, and have done much mischief; also many kinds of gambling, for the devil's agents are more numerous, if not more active, than those of Christ. These are not so many of our own countrymen; still there are a good many, and among them, I am ashamed to say, some who do harm. I hear terribly wicked words in broken English sometimes from poor donkey boys, who think it quite clever to be able to swear in English: who *but* Englishmen could have taught them this? And I have seen Englishmen sitting at a little table at the door of a provision shop, with two or three Egyptians drinking with them;—sad sight for missionaries, who leave their country, not for gain, like others, but to try and spread the truth, when they see the efforts made in the wrong direction, and especially if made by their own people. Few English reside here more than a term of years, and though each must leave his *mark* for good or bad, he affects the country or town less either way than if dwelling all his life here, and leaving a family to live after him. This is more the case with the other foreigners I spoke of, many of whom have never been out of Egypt at all. In general they have managed to lose what was good in European ways and habits, and to keep what signified very little (such as dress, etc.), or what was actually bad; and so with Eastern ways: they adopt just what might be let alone with advantage, and learn nothing of the really good things belonging to the Eastern nature or customs.

Their children grow up speaking the vulgar Arabic in addition to their own tongue, and clever in using all sorts of bad words, and in picking up gossip of the worst kind. They seem to lose the European horror of harem life, polygamy, etc., and that without the childish ignorance of the poor women of the country. I have had some in my school of these "Levantine" girls, as they are called, and generally found it scarcely possible to do them lasting good: the home influences were so contrary to all I wished to teach. An Arab school is not the thing for such children; they need a good Christian school, where only European languages are taught, under a pious and very strict Christian lady. At present there is nothing of the kind. I am speaking of free, or nearly free schools, as many of these families are poor, and even those who gain well in their business squander all their earnings in such a foolish way that there is nothing left to pay for proper schooling for their little ones. There are convents, where some girls of various nations are received, but they do not teach the Gospel there, and in many cases nothing at all except a few prayers to the Virgin and Saints, and a little sewing. A young woman of mixed race, whose widowed mother paid sixteen shillings a month—by hard work—for her schooling at a French convent, spent some years there, and came the other day to entreat me to write her a letter. She could not write, nor even read, in *any* language, though speaking several. The "good sisters," as they were called, had taught her nothing but prayers, as I said before.

Some of the Italians settled here are very bad indeed. I met, once, a woman, still young and handsome, at a railway station on the desert, who actually used the little Arabic she knew in trying to teach the poor peasant women (wives to the workmen who lived there) that "there was no God, and that when we die we turn to dust and never rise, and that man had no soul: it was all nonsense!" I heard the wretch, myself, on one occasion, and was told it was a common style of talk with her.

I just waited till she was out of the room, for I saw she had been drinking enough to excite her, and I wished to avoid a noise, etc.; then I began to talk to the poor woman she had addressed, and told her not to listen to this child of Satan, who *wanted* to believe there was no God because her own vile life went against His holy laws, and I warned her, of course, against listening to such terrible falsehoods. Alas! it is by no means the only time I have found foreigners deliberately trying to poison the minds of ignorant people, and to drag them, as it were, with themselves to perdition.

Ah! when will God's servants be roused to a sense of their great responsibility, and be as active for good as Satan's servants for evil?

Besides these Europeans, there are a large number of Syrians and Armenians settled here, some of whom hold important situations, and are much respected. There are also a large body of Jews, some from Europe, speaking the language of the country they came from, besides others, what are called Arabic Jews, who, having been here for centuries, speak only Arabic, and resemble in dress and some other things the people of the country. There are also, as I said before, many Turks resident here, but they are almost all either Government officials or wealthy Pachas.

Letter XII
The House of Mirth

You will, no doubt, like to hear something of the way in which the three events of such great importance in every country are celebrated in Egypt: marriages, births, and deaths. Every Bible student is aware that the festivals and the rejoicing at a marriage in the East in old times were much greater than even with us, though a wedding is always a "stir" in the quietest place. And like most of their customs this remains much as formerly, the only changes being such as change of religion would of necessity bring. As I before observed, in speaking about food, a father in the humbler classes of life often spends on a wedding feast for his son far more than he can afford, and is made poorer for years in some cases. The habits and ceremonies in all Eastern countries have great resemblance, even where not exactly the same, and we are constantly reminded in these matters of Scriptural allusions, though the accounts given of marriages there are not in Egypt. I cannot help thinking that it was the Mohammedan faith which brought in the custom of marrying girls while very young, often mere children, although the Copts do the same, but they have adopted a great many ways from their Mohammedan conquerors, and this may, perhaps, be one. At any rate, among the Jews it is evident, from various notices in the Old Testament, that the brides were young women, and not little girls, as they generally are here (not always, but in the greater number). For instance, Rebekah is asked by her brothers what she *chooses* to do, and her whole conduct is that of a person arrived at what we call years of discretion (Genesis 24:58); and Moses says of the daughters of Zelophehad, "Let them marry to whom they think best," etc. (Numbers 36:6). Here twelve and thirteen are the usual ages, and it is very common to see brides of ten, or even younger; they are a little forwarder, indeed, than children in the North, but only a year or two, and are really more childish in mind, from being without any education, than those who have been through the classes of a good infant school. Of course, it follows that the poor little things are not fit to "guide the house," as St. Paul says the young women ought to do (1 Timothy 5:14). Even a peasant's household, where so little is to be done, cannot be left to a mere child; so the young couple live, at least for some time, with the husband's parents, and in most cases till the old people die. The mother-in-law is generally disliked by her daughter-in-law, and tyrannizes over her; the happiest homes seem, with a few bright exceptions, those in which the old lady has been removed by death, or that the husband's business was such as to oblige him to live at a distance. The authority given to a mother-in-law is absolute: she can prevent her daughter-in-law from going out, and can, if a poor woman, beat and ill-use her as she likes, without interference. In the case of a powerful family belonging to the girl, this would not be tolerated, but life may be made very unhappy without blows. The degree of submission expected may be understood by the fact that if any lady (even one married several years, and whose husband may be kind and reasonable) wishes to visit me, she cannot do so, if she has a mother-in-law alive, unless she can obtain leave, just as if she were still a child. Israelitish matrons must have had much more freedom, as we see by the cases of the Shunammite (2 Kings 4) and of Abigail (1 Samuel 25), and others; and although the law of Moses allowed, "for the hardness of their hearts" (Deuteronomy 24:1–4; Matthew 19:7, 8), both divorce and polygamy, we may well believe neither was practised as commonly as they are now in the East, or women could not have held the position which they evidently did hold.

But we have not yet described the festivities which usher in this life of doubtful happiness for the young people. Nothing more plainly shows the importance of a wedding, and the rejoicings on the occasion of one, than the ordinary expression in speaking of it here; they do not say, in common talk, a *wedding*, but a *rejoicing*; even a baby will be saluted by, "To your rejoicing," which used to puzzle me sore at first, till I discovered it meant, May you be spared to have a wedding festivity by and by! They will say, "There is a rejoicing at such a one's next week," meaning his son or daughter is to be married.

When the parents have decided that they wish their son to marry (which in rich families is generally when he is still young, from seventeen to twenty, and sometimes younger, though this is not universal), they begin to look for a bride for him. The mother sets her female relatives to inquire among the neighbors, and an old woman, who lives by the business, acts as agent between the parties. In many families a relative is destined for the young man from childhood, but if this is not the case the bride-hunting goes on as I say. The young people have no voice in the matter at all, nor are they allowed to see each other till the knot is tied. The Coptic Egyptians follow the Moslems in this custom, and they are more to be blamed for it, because they *do* look on marriage as a sacred tie, and a lasting one, instead of letting it be broken for any trifle, as the law of Mohammed permits; and certainly it seems worse to bind two persons to each other, when it is an irrevocable tie, without letting them see and know something, at least, of one another. Much quarrelling and many very unhappy unions are the consequence of this foolish plan.

As soon as the affair is fixed between the two sets of parents, the marriage is generally hurried on as quickly as possible; if the family is wealthy, a few weeks are spent in turning the house upside down; with the poor, a few days to make a dress or two and prepare a feast is all that is needed. But with the rich, not a room is left out; white-washing and cleaning, making up of beds and sofas, and many such things, generally long wanted but which were put off till the occasion of the grand festival, are now done with as much speed as Eastern workmen can be got to put into their business. Meanwhile, women are seen running about, in pattens of wood, over the newly-washed floors; sewing-women, seated in corners, making new dresses for every member of the family, down to the baby. Negress slaves, looking as if basted freshly with oil, from their unwonted exertions (they are apt to be very fat), are scouring pans, and popping from one room to another, for any thing or nothing. The tinman sits in the court below with a pile of brass vessels which he is whitening inside, for the feast will require a great amount of cooking; and the master of the house has to order in great quantities of rice, sugar, clarified butter, and other articles, according to his means. All these details are seen alike in Christian and Moslem houses; it is chiefly when the ceremony comes that there is any difference in the arrangements. In poorer families the same goes on, only on a small scale, and as a rule you may say that every one spends more than is prudent on these occasions.

I am not going to give you every minute detail of the ceremonies of weddings, which would take too long and be tiresome, but the general plan is this: there are three days' feasting and rejoicing, the *days* being given to receiving visits, men and women separately, with pipes or cigars, and coffee for refreshments, and sitting on sofas if rich, on mats at the door if poor, and chatting. On the second day the bride is conducted to the bath by her mother and aunts, etc., in a sort of triumphal procession, and the women give a sort of shrill cry of joy, peculiar to the East, and used as a sign of great rejoicing, as they go along; one often hears it in the street, and sees a party of closely veiled figures, some with baskets on their heads, containing bridal gifts, etc. The bride is, of course, decked in her new attire; if she is very rich she wears a new dress several times in the course of the three days, but in ordinary families a rich brocaded silk of gay color is worn all the time, and she is laden with jewels; if not able to purchase all, her family borrow, and even hire, diamonds, rubies, and gold ornaments. Her fingers are covered with rings, and bunches of gilt tinsel paper are fixed at the sides of her head, the eyebrows painted in a black stripe, and she is ordered to close her eyes, or, at all events, to look down all the time, as she sits on a divan or sofa, and receives silently the salutations of the various female friends, for speaking is not allowed: she looks more like an idiot than a rational being. When she goes out for the processions, one to the bath, and the other to her new home, she is covered from head to foot with a large red Cashmere shawl, entirely hiding the face, not even the eyes appearing.

This is absolutely essential for an Eastern bride, so that the prints and pictures we see sometimes representing "an Eastern wedding procession," with the bride peeping out of her canopy and smiling at her friends, is totally incorrect, and ridiculous to those who have seen the real thing; but we shall be very glad when they learn that it is not necessary to hide their faces. A Coptic bride does not wear red as constantly as a Moslem one does; I have seen one in red, and another in white.

Musicians and singers form a necessary part of weddings. Where they can afford it, great sums are given to obtain celebrated female singers, though to European taste the Arab music is very monotonous indeed. The singing, in a rude, simple way, of peasant girls at work in the cotton fields, or Nile boatmen with the plash of their oars, is often very pleasing, as they have an ear for *time*, and sometimes very sweet voices, though apt to sing through their noses. But the more famous singers don't seem to us much better, and have not the open air to take off the nasal tone, nor the water as an accompaniment, and the being all in unison, with no treble and bass, *tires* the cultivated ear very much after a while. They delight in it themselves, however, and applaud with sighs and exclamations of satisfaction. The singers are placed up-stairs, but the windows open so that the men below can share the treat. Poorer people have a drum and reed pipe, at least, and seem to take great pleasure in them.

The whole day, or rather days, are given up to receiving guests and making merry; but the night is the grand time, the second especially, called the night of Henna. Henna is a certain tree, whose leaves, dried and pounded, are sold in quantities to dye the fingers of women, and sometimes their toes also, as they are usually barefoot in summer. Even if wealthy, it is only quite of late years that stockings are getting to be more worn. The bride is expected to have her hands dyed, both fingers and palms, and a paste, made of henna leaves with water, is prepared, and a great lump put in her hand. This was, at least, the old custom, every guest sticking on it a bit of money, and the collection thus made was for the female singers, the woman who dressed the bride's hair and attended her at the bath, etc.; whether all was given in this way, I am not sure. The hands and feet of the bride were, after the supper,—which at a very late hour followed the ceremony,—tied up with paste and left till morning, when they would be of a dark orange hue, which remains for several weeks, and only wears off by degrees. On the last day a Moslem bride is conducted through the streets in procession to the bridegroom's house, a canopy of red or pink being carried over her head, and her mother and female relatives walking beside and in front of her, while the men of her family and friends follow, and little boys with incense, and bride's-maids, who are generally quite little creatures, and all dressed in *red*, make the train a very lively one. It is always by day, and in summer the walk must be hot work, for they seem to go the longest circuit possible on purpose, and walk very slowly, often stopping to let the music which accompanies them be heard, and often men playing antics with sticks, pretending to fight, and jumping about, go before them. This is the real old Egyptian wedding procession, but quite of late years it is seen only among the humbler classes, as carriages having been introduced and become numerous, wealthy persons always now hire several for weddings, and stretch a red shawl over the top of one to show the red canopy. Of course it is much less original when all the train are packed up in carriages; and the peasant wedding is therefore more curious and amusing. The *prettiest* is, however, a country wedding, when, as is often the case, the bride's family come from some distance riding on camels. This is quite a picture to look at: two or three of these tall creatures, with a rude frame of wood fixed on their humps, upon which four women are seated,—often a baby or two beside,—and the rest either walking or on donkeys. The peasant bride and her mother or sister will usually wear a mantle of gay striped silk of a strong, soft texture, woven here, and which looks striking, as the others are all in their usual dark purple or black mantles.

The bridegroom's family, whether rich or poor, Copt or Moslem, have their part of rejoicing and feasting fully as much and even more; for a son's wedding is made more of than a daughter's, though both are considered great occasions. But they have their triumph separately, and only meet on the third and last day of the festival, when the feast is prepared at the house of the bridegroom, and the bride's father and friends partake below, while she and the female friends have their supper in an upper chamber. There is no wedding cake as in England, but all the favorite dishes are prepared, according to the means of the family. Many are extremely good, as the famous roast (or rather baked) lamb, stuffed with rice, nuts, pistachios, and other things, and which every European who has tasted it approves. Some of their dishes are less to our taste, from the great amount of butter and grease used in them. The poorer people think more of quantity, and serve up boiled mutton and fowls, rice, etc., in heaps to their friends.

The only *legal* part of the Moslem wedding is a contract made by the fathers or guardians before a judge, quite privately, no guests being present, only the needful witnesses. Certain chapters of the Koran are read, I believe, by a Mollah, who answers in some respects to a priest, though not by any means in all. The bridegroom is expected to go to the Mosque before his wedding, and sometimes has a train of friends to accompany him in procession. As to the bride, religion seems not to enter into her share of the wedding at all, and there are no mutual vows of love before God, as with us.

With Copts of course it is different; they have a very long religious ceremony, sometimes at the church, but sometimes, in Cairo, the whole is performed by the Patriarch, and several priests who assist, at the house of the bridegroom. The prayers are in Coptic, and psalms are chanted in this now dead language, none of the hearers understanding a word; but some portions of Scripture and exhortations are read in Arabic. At one part of the ceremony crowns of gold (or gilding) are placed on the heads of the bride and groom, and at another an embroidered silk shawl is thrown over both their heads as they sit on a sofa together. It is a very long affair, as is the case in the Greek Church, which the Coptic resembles very much. The Coptic procession is at night, or late in the evening, and looks very pretty when it is a walking procession, all lighted up with torches. There are evening processions also at Moslem weddings, but the bride is not with them; hers is always at midday or the afternoon. I have seen very pretty-looking processions of a bridegroom and his friends by night going through the streets, each holding a bunch of flowers and green sprigs, with a lighted taper fixed in the middle. They all wear their richest dresses and turbans; the bridegroom in red-striped vest and crimson outer robe usually; and the effect, as they march slowly along chanting with the light in their hands, is very curious and picturesque. It is to be hoped that those who have adopted European dress have given up processions; for men in our garb certainly do not show well in such sort of things, and the mixture of East and West is sometimes very incongruous, or as one might say, in homely language, two sides that do not match.

At last all is over, and the families must, I think, be glad to rest, especially the mother, after the din of native music, talking, saluting, attending to guests, cooking, and all the fatigue. For three nights, mother, aunts, and sisters have only snatched a little sleep on a sofa in some corner by turns! When the wedding is in summer, it *is* an exhausting affair, though the people of the country do not feel the heat as we do; but the rooms are crammed to suffocation, and, however large, have too many guests for comfort, and many of the middle-class houses have rooms quite too small for such a climate, the modern ones especially: *old* Egyptian houses, on the contrary, have usually two or three very large rooms, and several little ones only used for sleeping, or keeping stores, etc.

The crowd of women is increased by their almost all bringing their slaves with them, as well as *all* their children, little and big, so that, in spite of open windows, the faces of most (if it be a summer wedding) are trickling with moisture. The men who sit outside are better off in this respect.

The grand day is at length at an end, and the family resume ordinary life, though a bride's friends usually call on her after a few days, if not of the laboring class, who cannot afford to sit stuck up in fine clothes, doing nothing all day.

"And how is your daughter?" I said to a Moslem lady, in very good worldly circumstances, who had recently been to pay a visit to a married daughter, whose wedding took place about two months before. "Well, I thank you, she kisses your hand," replied the parent, giving a sigh, and looking far from cheerful. "I hope she is happy." "So-so, the man is not better than most, he is obstinate" (has a hard head was the expression used). "Is her mother-in-law kind?" "Hum, not very; and then his sisters are also there," shrugging her shoulders: "she is not happy, and she does not like their cookery!" I could not help thinking of "a dinner of herbs, where love is" (Proverbs 15:17).

There are more cheering instances, certainly. I know one young woman whose mother-in-law and sister are extremely fond of her, but they seem (for I know them but little) to be very amiable themselves, and the young wife is of a particularly lively temper, and easy to please. The greater number that I see do not appear happy; sometimes content because they make the best of what *is*; but few are happy in the real sense of the word, and I know many cases of terrible misery,—not, observe, from husbands of the lowest and worst of the people,—such are to be found, alas! in every country,—but where they are of the respectable classes, and well considered: for example, a very sweet young girl was lately married to a man who was very well known to have beaten his first wife till she died from the injuries, and to have bribed those who ought to have punished him, yet he found no difficulty in obtaining a third wife (the second he had divorced), and that from a respectable family.

Then there is a long train of wretchedness which polygamy brings. "How is your hand so hurt?" I asked a poor woman once, whose hand I was binding up for her, at her request. "My husband did it with a stick; he was beating me," she answered. "What for?" She held up three fingers of the other hand in reply, and then said, "There are *three* of us."

I frequently hear sad domestic histories, which show the

misery produced by this custom. We know that, although *allowed* in barbarous times of old, it never was productive of comfort and peace, but quite the contrary; and so it is now, and always will be. A few there are, who, not from poverty, but from their own conscience and sense, will only have one wife, and surely a blessing will attend them for this. But they are still quite exceptions.

Among native Christians, of course, polygamy is not allowed; but the early marriage of the girls, and the undue power given to the mother-in-law, and the want of previous acquaintance, all combine with ignorance to make happy marriages not very common among them either. If they could only learn (but too many neglect it, with us, who have an open Bible, and can read it), "The woman that feareth the Lord, *she* shall be praised" (Proverbs 31:30), how different might things be!

When the family begins there is generally much joy, for children are earnestly desired and dearly loved in the East; but there is less of external rejoicing than with us, as there is (among Moslems) no ceremony answering to baptism with us, and we must always bear in mind, in speaking of Egypt, that, though a very important portion of the nation, the Copts, or native Christians, are a very small part, numerically, of the nation: they agree with their Moslem neighbors in letting the terror of that unseen evil, "the eye," about which I told you in a former letter, spoil much of the young mother's comfort, as well as of the female relatives, who, of course, cluster about her on this occasion. There is a sort of suppressed happiness, and a fear of *showing* satisfaction, on every face when one goes to pay the customary visit of congratulation to a neighbor when a first-born is given to the household. Not unfrequently, the grandmother and aunts will pretend it is a girl when really a boy, for several days, because "the eye" is more likely to strike one of the nobler sex, though girls are by no means supposed to be secure from its influence. They are very fond, in general, of their little girls, but *prize* boys very much more, and are quite unhappy if Providence deny a son, although there may be no inheritance for him but rags!

I once knew a young woman whose husband, quite early in their married life, divorced her, for no reason but her baby being a girl. She told me this while showing me an uncommonly pretty and vigorous-looking little thing of six months old, and said she had to go back to her mother, as he would not support her. I must add, in fairness, that her husband was a bad character; he was a stone-cutter, and was afterwards detected in stealing, and banished; but the fact of the young wife and the baby-girl shows the kind of feeling prevailing with many.

A far more respectable man, a butcher, well-to-do in his line, has a nice daughter at my school, but this girl has had in succession no less than four step-mothers. All were divorced for the same cause, that they had only daughters, and it appeared as if God punished him by denying his wish,—to this date he has no boy.

But to return to the newly-arrived baby. When going to visit the mother, which it is considered quite unkind not to do,—if it be a first especially,—the neighbors and relatives all put on an air almost of mystery, and the new mother is not forward to display her treasure; on the contrary, it is very often hidden away in a corner and covered up.

"How is the bridegroom?" you may say, this being the term applied to a baby-boy, in politeness. "God preserve him."

"He kisses your hand, we thank God," replies the

mother, or rather, in the case of a very young person, the grandmother, for the poor little creature hardly knows what to make of her new honors, and is so tutored and commanded by the old woman that she seems like a puppet. The female guests are always curious, of course, and slyly peep to see the little one in his nook, and at last one summons courage to lift the handkerchief from his face, but she must not say, "What a fine boy!" or "What pretty eyes!" or "How like he is to his mother!" etc. She turns to another friend, and observes, "An ugly little thing!" "He is very brown" (a fair skin is from its rarity admired), says the next; "Not in the least nice!" adds a third, nodding sagely. The last remark is apt to be too true, as he is not clean, and his eyes have been daubed with a mixture of oil, salt, and onion-juice, with a view to strengthen them (by trying what they *can* endure, I presume), so that the poor lamb is *not* very nice certainly, unless he belongs to an exceptional mother. There are a few such. One I know refused to let her baby's eyes be meddled with, and persisted in washing them and its body with pure water, and is rewarded by the healthy appearance of her dear pretty little girl; but then she was not a *young* mother,—she had a great tall girl at my school for years, and her little *Zanuba* was a late blossom. The youthful mother is so completely ruled by the mother-in-law that she cannot free herself from these absurd customs.

While these polite little observations are being made, the slave, if they have one, and, if not, a female relative, presents, instead of the usual little cups of coffee, a drink, made for the occasion, of hot water with spice and sugar, and chopped *nuts* floating in it. The friends generally bring some small present, especially a muslin handkerchief, to throw over the baby's head, or a piece of colored print or silk, etc., according to means.

The Moslem babe is named without any special ceremony. They have a great variety of names, the meaning of which is thought more of than with us, who merely choose a name as sounding well or belonging to a friend or relation. The prime favorites with boys are names which have some reference to their Prophet, either to his supposed titles and attributes, or those of his relations, Mohammed himself being of course the commonest of all. Some names have a pretty and poetical meaning, as, "Servant of the Light" (Abdel Noor), "Servant of the Lofty One," etc. Hassan, Hosseen, Alee, and Ahmed are the most frequent, however, being names of the Prophet's friends and relations, and answer to our John, Tom, and William, etc. Girls are very often called after the Prophet's daughter and wives, Zeynab, Aysha (or in Egypt Ay*u*sha, the *u* being diminutive), and Fatmeh or Fat*u*ma. These are the commonest, but they have a great variety of names, some of which are very pretty both in sound and meaning. A girl is always supposed to have a name implying something pleasant, "the sweet," "the pretty," "the gentle," "the clever," "the gazelle" (this animal being celebrated for its beauty and gentleness), "the flower," "the jasmine," "the tuberose," etc., or again, "the princess," "the queen."

I must here tell you of a curious superstition about names, especially, I think, girls' names. We sometimes get a little scholar, or meet a girl among acquaintances, who has a very uncouth and clumsy name, such as "Mother of Mohammed," "Mother of Goodness," "Mother of the Lofty One." They do not admire this sort of name at all, but give it in the hope that God will be induced by this to spare the child, the mother having lost several before her!

"Why did you choose so ugly a name?" I asked a Bedouin woman at the Pyramids; not one of the poor little colonist

Bedouins in wigwams, but a fine, strong, handsome woman, living in a stone hut, and well off in her way. She had a very pretty little girl of a year old on her lap, and told me she was called *Um el Kheyr,* "Mother of Goodness."

"I know it is ugly," said she, "but I want her to live."

"How will an ugly name make her live?"

"Why, you see, I had two sweet girls before her, and called them Fatmeh and Zanuba, and they both died, so I called this one by the name of Mother of Goodness, so that God perhaps will spare her;" and the poor dear thing looked at me so piteously that I felt tears come in my eyes. I tried to show her that it was not a name that God cared for, but that she must pray to Him to keep her darling if He saw fit, and spent some time talking with her, and reading some passages of the Gospel to show how God is *love.* I have not been able to find her since, but she declared that she saw things differently, and would trust only in God in future. May the seed cast on the waters be blessed for His name's sake!

The Copts have a curious superstition about names, different from this. They light three wax candles or tapers, and give each a name, a saint's name being always at least one of the three, and the one that is last in going out is the child's name. The patron saint of Copts is St. George. This name, which they call *Gergas*, is therefore the commonest among them. Many names, however, are common both to Copts and Moslems, as some of the patriarchs' names, Abraham, etc., but *Ishmael* is only used by Moslems, because they think the son of Hagar was Abraham's promised seed, thus strangely perverting the Scripture narrative. Many foreign (i.e., Greek) names are in use among Copts, from the saints they venerate being Greeks; others will choose Italian names if they belong to the small division of Copts who have joined the Roman Catholic Church. But the Arab names suit better in general with the language. They baptize their children in infancy generally at the church, and by immersion; the ceremony is very nearly the same as in the Greek Church.

Letter XIII
The House of Mourning

"*Man is as a flower of the field,* which to-day is, and to-morrow is cast into the oven" (see Psalm 103:15 and Matthew 6:30). While one house is full of joy and merriment, the next is plunged in woe, "because man goeth to his long home, and the mourners go about the streets" (Ecclesiastes 12:5).

This is true, literally, in the East, where mourning is so public and so local. If one is walking or riding, and meets a funeral procession, it is not a silent black troop as in Europe, but a long train of Mollahs chanting, and numbers of women uttering at intervals the most piercing shrieks and cries, so that all down the street the sounds of woe are heard. When I lived in a narrow street of the city, I used to realize the awful woe that fell on this very land on the death of the first-born,—"And there was a great *cry* in Egypt" (Exodus 12:30),—for sometimes in the silence of night a sudden cry in one of the houses near would rouse me from sleep, and the cry would be followed by others, shrieks and wild lamentations, and sounds as of women beating on their breasts and nearly beside themselves, and many a prayer has gone up for those poor sorrow-laden creatures, who could not say of those they wept for, "We know they are with Jesus." Of course there are families where there is not very deep affection, as in the not rare case of an unkind husband, but the crying and screaming, if not so heart-felt, would go on just the same, because it is a *custom*, and the household are assisted in its performance by hired women, who are always sent for on such occasions. This was evidently the custom also among the Jews: "Call hither the mourning women that they may come,—let them make haste and take up a wailing for us, that our eyes may run down with tears, and our eyelids gush out with waters (Jeremiah 9:17, 18). These professed mourners, by their doleful chants, in which they praise the departed, and bring forward every thing likely to affect the friends, excite them to more violent grief, and when they are for a moment calmer from actual exhaustion, and are sitting quiet, they set them off again, till it is a wonder the poor wives and mothers are not completely worn out.

There is no word like that of a Christian friend or minister, who points the afflicted upwards, to where Jesus the Captain of our Salvation is making ready the many mansions, where His servants hope one day to rest from sorrow with Him and with those who have "departed this life in His faith and fear"; no one to say "darkness may endure for a night, but joy cometh in the morning" (Psalm 30:5). Nothing more convinces me of the *very* small degree of comfort which the Moslem faith affords, than the absence of any consolation to the bereaved. Their book tells of future state, indeed, but at the time of a funeral the females of a family especially are left utterly without a word of comfort; the chanting women lament the *past*, but I never heard that they had a word to say about the *future*. Many Moslems die in great peace and calmness, but some may have a ray of light sent in some way we do not know; others, *numbers*, I fear, are in a state of false peace, and resting on sand, though they know it not. A man may die in a comfortable security that he leaves his children a good farm, not knowing that there is a flaw in the title-deeds; such is the case of all, in whatever country and whatever religion they profess, whose hope of future happiness is not resting on the promise of God as given in His revealed Word.

Jesus said, "I am the resurrection and the life" (John 11:25), "I am the way" (John 14:6), and again, "I am the *door*" (John 10:9). If there were any other resurrection, any other way, any other door, would He who is *truth* and love have said these words so plain that none can mistake them?

"My little one is gone, and *where?*" cried a weeping mother one day to me, stretching out her arms with a gesture that said a great deal more than words could do. How I thanked God that I could say (as I dared not have said in most cases) that I felt *sure* her little daughter was with the Lord Jesus, for that she loved and believed in Him truly, and that He had doubtless received her in His arms above. She had been a little scholar in my school from four years old up to near eleven, and I had taught her to repeat the first text when she could but lisp the holy words. Very early she had shown that interest in Scripture, and by actions proved that she really believed the Gospel. This is years ago; I have often visited the mother, but though she knows what her child believed, she as yet remains stubborn in unbelief, and tries to put away the thought of the future. However, I do not despair, and still hope she may one day follow where the dear child is gone before.

Another scholar, who died at the age of sixteen, as nearly as we can tell, was a firm believer in the Gospel; I used daily to read to her in her illness, which was not very long, and always found her trusting fully in the merits and blood of Christ, in the midst of great weakness and suffering. "Do ask that He may take me *soon!*" she said one day, with childlike confidence of going to the Lord straight, and she gave me repeated assurances that she had no fear in death, and knew she was forgiven.

I was reminded strongly of Jairus's daughter (Mark 5:22–43) when I saw this dear girl surrounded by the women "wailing and weeping and making a noise," exciting the poor mother's grief by piteous laments. "I thought to have decked thee for a marriage feast one day, my daughter," cried one, "and now must I deck thee for the grave,—so young and so good? Ah! my daughter,—ah black day! my woe, my sorrow!" then a chorus of shrieks interrupted her. In the midst of this tumult, robed as for a bridal, in red, and adorned with jewels, lay the calm, peaceful, wasted face of her whose happy spirit had fled where she would never again hear sounds of woe! The last words she had heard on earth had been the words of the twenty-third Psalm, which I repeated to her: "And I shall dwell in the house of the Lord for ever." I repeated them twice, adding, "For *ever*, my daughter,—for ever with the Lord." I had seen her eye follow me, though no longer able to speak; but the women thought she would linger some hours yet, and had not therefore brought a Mollah to read or recite prayers, as they do very frequently, if not always, with departing persons of respectable families. I had, however, scarcely reached the end of the street, when a girl ran after me, saying, "She is gone!" I returned, and found the scene I have just described, and could not but say in my heart, "The damsel is not dead, but sleepeth." We have reason to hope that the effect produced by her life and death—but the former especially—has not been lost in her family.

You will naturally ask what the men are about during these noisy lamentations. They leave the outcries mostly to the women, and walk silently in the funeral procession. This takes place within twelve hours after decease, which is only right in such a climate.[1] Moslems use a bier covered with a red cloth, and a raised piece of wood at the head, also covered with a red shawl, has the turban (if a man) of the dead fixed to it; if a woman, the female head-dress of little gold coins, fastened to black silk cords hanging from a small red cap, takes the place of the manly turban. This cap and coin ornament is now going out of use a good deal, but is generally displayed at a funeral; probably one is hired for the occasion in many cases. They, i.e., the Moslems, bury without a coffin, and dressed in their best clothes; in very rich families, a person is sometimes buried with silk garments and jewels of value,—a very bad custom, as robberies of tombs, in spite of the superstitious dread of evil spirits, etc., do sometimes take place.

The family and friends, more or less, according to circumstances, accompany the funeral; in the case of a Sheik, or any great man, flags are carried, and incense borne by boys from the Moslem school, and an immense number of men follow the train, but, in ordinary burials, flags, etc. are dispensed with. Men are taken to the Mosque, however, and certain prayers and passages of the Koran recited, after which they proceed to the cemetery (children, and even women, unless of distinguished family, are taken straight to the burial-place, and no special religious ceremony performed). The Mollahs and some boys with the men friends go first, chanting, and the women follow

[1] Sometimes, however, they do not wait half the allotted time, and risk burying people alive. A carpenter told me lately an old Copt was just going to be fixed in his coffin, when he spoke, and proved, of course, to be alive.

with handkerchiefs, generally blue ones, in their hands, which they twist into a kind of rope, and pull as they walk, sometimes brandishing them over their heads; it seems to me to be a sort of imitation of the old custom of rending the garments; Egyptians sometimes tear their clothes still (not only in grief, but in anger), but it is not a regular part of funeral observance, and I fancy the neighbors have no idea of sacrificing their clothes as well as their time. They are called on so often, being expected to attend the funeral of the most distant relation or friend, if within reach of a walk, as well as of neighbors, that it loses a great deal of the poorer women's time, and if they really tore their clothes, they would always be in rags!

The chanting is chiefly about Mohammed, the apostle of God, as they say, and the men's voices are often fine-sounding and pleasing, though we should like different words. It is interrupted by the cries of the hired women from behind, and occasionally by bursts of genuine grief from the relations, as "Oh my brother!" "Oh my son!" "Oh sister, sister!" reminding one forcibly of the words of Jeremiah in denouncing the wicked king Jehoiakim, "They shall not lament for him, saying, Ah my brother! or, Ah sister! or, Ah Lord! or, Ah his glory!" (Jeremiah 22:18).

On their return, the friends sit for some time with the bereaved family, only men and women apart as usual, and the women meet to cry every week on a certain day till forty days are past.

It is odd to hear the women crying periodically in this way till these days are ended, and not unfrequently to be told, as soon as they are finished, that the husband (if it be the case of a wife who is taken) is already looking for a bride, and will soon prepare for the wedding.

A mother does not forget so soon, but she tries to

banish what she has so little comfort under. I knew one (doubtless she was one among many) who went the long and fatiguing pilgrimage to Mecca,[1] a journey partly by sea and partly riding on a camel through burning deserts,—no light affair for a woman of at least sixty years old; yet she did it, and, as she confessed to me, more for the sake of the entire change than for religious motives: probably both had some share in her mind. Yet she might have taken some better comfort, for her son, whose death was so heavy a trial to her, had not died without leaving some cause to hope that he found peace. They had sent to me in the idea that I could give some bodily remedy, and when I found the poor lad (he was about eighteen) was already past this, and that to urge them to call a doctor would be useless, as already mortification in his back had begun,—I asked leave to read to him, and for several days tried to bring before him a few simple texts, especially this, "Behold the Lamb of God, which taketh away the sins of the world" (John 1:29). I tried to explain it as clearly as I could, and we prayed for him at home. He listened earnestly, and used to say, "Read, read!" when the women neighbors, bigoted and ignorant, tried to hinder me, and rudely told me no one wanted books there.

After a few days, in which the suffering lessened, so that he had but little pain, he suddenly had a fit of internal spasms of some sort. The neighbor who told me said he had just been telling her that "the lady had been reading him such *sweet* words, such *good* words;" the pain there stopped him, and he went on groaning for a while, then looked up, exclaimed, "Lord, make me to follow Thee!" and expired.

The mother and sister, etc. had just returned from the

[1] Mecca is the holy city of the Moslems, and it is thought a pious act to visit it.

funeral when I went. I found all the women—at least fifty in number—seated on mats in the narrow lane where they lived, which was not a thoroughfare. I sat down beside the poor women, and after expressions of sympathy offered to read her a few words of God's *own* comfort, as I told her, out of the Book.

"Yes, yes, read me the book my son loved," said she, and listened with quieter tears while I read in a low voice, close to her ear, some verses suited for the case, and easy to understand. But presently a great, rough-looking woman near us got sight of the book, and said, rudely, "Go away, you and your Christian book; we want no books, we want to cry!" I tried to pacify her with the soft answer that turneth away wrath, but with no great success. She gave a nudge, as I thought, to the hired mourners, who set up a louder chant than before, and echoes of howling and shrill crying nearly deafened me. Then suddenly pausing, the wailing woman said, in her usual voice, "I am not going to cry any more unless you give me something," and a brown, wrinkled hand was held out, and several put small coins into it,—not much, for it was a poor district.

I did not approve of paid laments; nevertheless, not to offend them, as it was not a sinful though a silly custom, I put in a trifle of about the value of threepence, and then rose to take leave. Certainly it was the first time I had ever been actually sitting on the ground in a street before, but, as I remarked, it was not a thoroughfare, and there were neither vehicles nor passers-by. The scene was singular, the women rocking to and fro with their blue handkerchiefs, wailing and sobbing; and then those who came only for kindness, getting tired, would turn to one another and begin to whisper gossip.

It was not unlike an Irish wake, only the worst parts of

those wakes (which I hope will soon be entirely things of the past) are wanting in an Egyptian funeral celebration; no strong drink is produced, and no mixing of young people for games and amusements: it is a wailing time and nothing else with them.

A very singular custom is observed in some families, both Moslems and Copts, at the decease of a chief person, as the master of the house, or a grown-up son, etc.; this is a kind of dance held by the women and their friends, who all assemble in the best room of the house, and dance in a circle, with a curious little jumping motion, slapping their own faces at the same time. They carry on this till they become perfectly exhausted, and return home with cheeks swelled, and painful and violent headaches for the remainder of the day; the slapping is sometimes observed without the dance, and in that case they merely sit on the floor rocking themselves, and beating their faces, alternating this exercise with groans and tears. The dance is said to be more frequent in Upper Egypt, but it is performed here very often, and in highly respectable families.

The Coptic burial ceremonies are, of course, different from the Moslems, and resemble those of the Greek Church, but what we may call the *domestic* ceremonies are very nearly the same.

The great Moslem cemetery of Cairo is on the borders of the desert, where is abundance of space for the purpose. Every Friday women may be seen going to visit the tombs of some dead relative, not that they go every week, but Friday is the "visiting day" for the tombs. A little girl came to ask leave to be absent from school one Friday, because her mother was going to take her to visit her grandmother. I happened to ask where she lived, and was amazed to hear the grandmother was dead years ago; "We are going to her tomb," the child at last explained. At the "Great" and "Lesser" festivals, as the two principal Mohammedan feasts are called, the visiting the tombs of their relatives is a necessary part of the proceedings. The Lesser feast, which comes first, has most of this visiting; it is customary then for the people to go very early, often at daybreak, carrying branches of palm and myrtle trees, and sometimes "hebbuk," or sweet basil; these green boughs are laid on the tombs, and certain prayers recited by the sheiks, or the men themselves if they are able. Every one is in his best and gayest clothes, and the scene is extremely pretty,—the road crowded with men, women, and children, all clean, and in lively-colored garments, carrying their boughs, and sometimes flowers, and hastening along in the early sunshine. It seems any thing but a sorrowful day,—sweetmeat and fruit sellers are in numbers, every one brings bread, etc., and they eat and drink and are merry. The solemnity of a cemetery does not hinder the great swings, which are always erected in the neighborhood, and where not only children but grown men delight in swinging. It is *queer* to us, but it is only Christians (I mean by that *real* believers in Christ, as the "Author and Finisher" of our faith, the A and the Z, the beginning and the end)—it is only *such* who can understand *solemnity* joined to *cheerfulness* (I think so at least), and who can feel the *link* between sorrow and joy,—the tear and smile meeting as they hold sweet converse about the blessed ones who are gone before. With the people here (as, alas! with many others), if they think at all of those they have lost, until time has, as it *must, deadened* the feeling,—it is with bitter, often with angry grief. Then they try to forget, as soon as the violence of sorrow has worn itself out, because their views of the future *cannot* satisfy the higher part of our nature. Many of the women have so vague and dim a notion about the soul, that they have been said to believe women *have* no souls. This is not part of the Moslem religion, however, though many among peasant females will say, "Really, I don't know if we have any souls, or what they are;" but a woman who has any claim to being "religious," and has learnt some prayers out of their book by heart, will always tell you she believes the faithful go to Paradise. This is not the Paradise spoken of in the Bible; we hear Eden, where our first parents lived before the fall, spoken of as Paradise, although not in the Scriptures, where the only mention of Paradise is in the Gospel of Luke, when our Saviour tells the repentant thief that he should be with Him "to-day in Paradise" (Luke 23:43), and again in the Epistle of St. Paul to the Corinthians (2 Corinthians 12:4), and in the Book of Revelation, where it is said that the tree of life is in the midst of the "Paradise of God" (Revelation 2:7). It is doubtless this mention of the tree of life that made people give the name of Paradise to Eden, where we first hear of the tree of life. But there sin and Satan entered, and in the Paradise where the Lord Jesus is with His redeemed, neither of these can come; little as we are told, we may be sure it is a glorious place, where souls released from the burden of these infirm bodies will rest with their Saviour, awaiting a yet more entire and perfect glory, when, after the resurrection, their sanctified bodies will clothe the souls, and so shall they be, as the Apostle says, for ever with the Lord (1 Thessalonians 4:17). Very different is the Paradise which is invented by man; the descriptions of the Mohammedan place of happiness are of the earth, earthy indeed (1 Corinthians 15:47),—coarse sensual enjoyments, eating and drinking constantly, without becoming ill from excess, having a multitude of wives, and many other details, some quite absurd, as the gigantic size they expect to attain, etc., all show a childish and unspiritual idea of happiness. When we compare these descriptions with the few but glorious words granted to us by God of the *true* abode of the blessed, the difference is—just what we might expect between God's words and man's. "God Himself shall be with them" (Revelation 21:3); there shall be no more sorrow nor pain,—God Himself wiping away tears from their eyes; the white robes clean and pure (showing that all sin is washed away),—why, every *word* is *weighted* with glory, if one may dare to use such an expression! Then those few but precious words in Thessalonians, about being caught up to meet the Lord in the air *together*,—all who loved and were one in Him on earth, to be *together* with Him in happiness,—"for ever with the Lord,"—what can equal that? Ah! my friends, let us thank God for His Gospel, and *accept* it for ourselves, and then let all who have accepted it help me to pray for the poor Egyptians, who have only a false peace to delude their souls, and who sorrow over their dear ones as they that have no hope!

Letter XIV

Nile Trips

No doubt you have often heard of travellers who visit Egypt "going on the Nile," but as it is not very likely you will go yourselves, you may like to have a better idea of what it means than you can get by that rather indistinct description of the journey! In one of my earlier letters, I told you that many remains of the old Egyptian Pagan temples, and of the buildings raised by their kings in old times for memorials of their greatness, were still to be seen. The finest of these are at a distance from Cairo, but near the river; many persons who are interested in ancient things go to visit these curious ruins, and what makes their attraction much greater is the mild winter climate, which suits many delicate people. So, some for pleasure, and some for health, a great many travellers go every winter up the river. There are small-sized steamers where parties can be taken up at less expense than separate boats, but wealthy families usually prefer the comfort of these last. The private boats are sailing boats, and are called generally by the Arab name *Daha-beeyeh* (mispronounced in various ways by the new arrivals). They are large enough to contain a cabin for eating and sitting in, and some little sleeping-berths, more or less, as may be. A native captain (often a Nubian) and seven or eight men manage the boat, which has a large sail, of the shape of a bird's wing, and they are very clever in taking this sail down quickly in change of weather, which is needful on the Nile, where are many dangerous currents, but, with a steady captain, it is extremely rare to meet with accident.

The travellers take provisions and every thing they want, but can buy fowls, eggs, milk, and sometimes a lamb, as they go along. The voyage to Luxor, where some of the chief ruins are found, takes three or four weeks, and those who go as far as into Nubia must be absent, going and coming, for more than two months. My personal experience of Nile voyages is nothing like this, being only short trips on one of the smaller boats, hired for a fortnight, or even less, and only going a short distance. But as I and my friends go for the sake of bringing the Gospel to some of the villages on the river, our employment is so deeply interesting that no ruined temples could delight us so much, for man is a *ruin* himself, ruined by sin and Satan, and only the knowledge of a Saviour can raise him out of that ruined condition. It is only scattered seed, of course, that can be spread in short visits like these, but we have cause to hope that some is not lost.

I have a number of old journals, letters, and rough notes, made at different times of these voyages, and I will make a few short extracts from some of them, to give you some idea of the places and the work.

One fine, bright, breezy winter day, more like May in England, or something between May and October, Mr. Shakoor and his brother were seated on the deck of our boat, a well-filled bag of books and tracts beside them, which they were sorting, pausing now and then to look at the fair scenes through which we passed, as our white-winged boat skimmed cheerily along the river; and the ladies of the party, having settled their tiny cabins, sat also on deck, noting all they saw. The banks are not green in general, nor flowery,—the inundation prevents that, making a fresh bank every year,—and yet there is a great deal of beauty; the clear air and brilliant sun make *every thing* beautiful, in fact, and the groups of palms are a delight to the eye. Fields of bright green clover and young corn reach as far as eye can see on one side, on the other a range of cliffs, sometimes high, sometimes low, barren, and dry; but their yellow and white rocks take wonderful colors, in the sunset especially. Little villages dot the coast, some all among palm-trees, others with only a few standing up like sentinels among the low mud dwellings; here and there a little grove of gum-arabic trees grow near the river on a raised pathway, and as the sky grows red with the evening light, and the sun sinks behind golden clouds, troops of peasants are seen on this same high pathway, driving their buffaloes and cows from the pasture, and shepherds with large flocks of goats. It is customary (and is safest) to moor the boats at night, so we draw up to shore, and are soon made fast to a peg driven into the earth. A number of men, wrapped in mantles, of brown goat's-hair, or wool, are seated on the bank; one or two are still at their evening prayers, kneeling and touching the ground with their heads, then standing, then kneeling again, and all the while repeating the Moslem form of prayer. They mean well, poor men, and we respect their honest wish to do what they fancy pleases God, but that is not *prayer* in the right sense of the word. One of the missionaries is now seated on the bank beside some of them, and, after friendly salutations and kind remarks, begins to inquire if any can read, and, by degrees, gets into a very interesting conversation. Meantime, I am watching the women who come to draw water. Sunset is not a leisure time for them, as it is with the cultivators of the soil; they have to draw water for supper, and are in great haste. It is pretty to see how nimbly their bare feet descend the steep bank, and how rapidly they lower the immense jars from their heads, tuck the loose dress round their legs, wade into the stream, wash the jar or pitcher, then fill, and *haul* it to shore, and then help each other to hoist it on the head again, and walk up the bank with firm, quick steps: no time to listen to strangers now, but my turn will come to-morrow.

It gets dark quickly in Egypt, and when the moon is up it is apt to be cold at this time of year, so we retreat to our cabin for tea, and then have family worship, in which earnest prayer is made that the Lord's word may be blessed to some of these poor souls.

Well wrapped in my cloak, I am on deck as soon as the sun is up, indeed, have been trying to paint its gorgeous colors in my sketch-book from the cabin window, before the dazzling flood of light burst from the long line of gold-edged clouds, and made the calm waters shine and shimmer, so that I could no longer gaze steadily at them. We call to the servant to give us breakfast quickly, as we want to go on land, and soon we are speeding up the bank and entering a grove of palm-trees, which surround the large mud village, which has, we are told, a thousand inhabitants. The green corn looks lovely, growing under the light shade of the palms, but the heaps of dust and rubbish which are in and around the village are neither pretty nor savory. A good many of the peasants have already come from their early morning work, and are taking a rest, some eating a piece of dry bread as they sit in the sun, with their backs against a low mud wall, some smoking from a long pipe handed round among them; one or two are spinning the brown wool of their sheep with a simple distaff, made of two little sticks, and a spindle which dances about as they twist the thread. The missionaries exchange a look, as if to say, "Here is our work," and soon are in conversation with a group of peasants; then they are invited to the house of one of the chief men, and before long are seated in a large sort of shed, with about thirty or more men in white turbans and goat's-hair mantles squatted around, listening with faces of wonder and attention to the words of Him who spoke as never yet man spake. Like the seed scattered by the sower, much may fall on the wayside, or among thorns, but not *all*, though till the last day we *may* not perhaps know which fell on good ground.

Meanwhile, Mrs. Shakoor and I are seeking for the women; they are dawdling about at the doors of their huts, doing nothing for the most part. The water was fetched at sunrise, and it is now nearly ten o'clock, they have nothing therefore to do. Breakfast was a piece of bread and perhaps some milk or curds, taken whenever they felt hungry; the children had crawled off the mats where they slept when they chose, and no dressing and washing was performed except that each peasant woman washed hands and feet in the Nile when drawing water (for in this point they are cleaner than towns-people of the same class). Their heads look as if it were months since they had seen a comb, and the children are mostly in rags, but look healthier than those in Cairo, for the air of the Nile is very fine.

After a little chat about their babies, and other matters likely to interest them, we get a little opening for the "Book," which of course is with us.

Circumstances after a time prevented our going on these Nile trips for several years, but in the month of February, 1878, my sister accompanied me, with Mrs. Shakoor's brother[1] and sister on a short, but as it proved deeply-interesting voyage. To my great delight time had not taken away all recollection of former visits; on the contrary, I was recognized by several persons in different villages, and most affectionate inquiries made as to why for so long a time we had not come. We had, at one village especially, little meetings nearly all day, and our tracts and gospels were eagerly asked for by those who could read. These were chiefly young men or boys; to the women we read and talked, and tried to make them understand a little at least of the love of God in Christ.

A great deal depends, humanly speaking, on the sheik of a village, as respects the treatment of strangers; the sheiks here have a great degree of power, which seems to be partly religious and partly legal. If a man is to be taken as a conscript for the army, it is to the sheik of his village that the Government officers apply, and if any thing goes wrong in a place, it is the sheik who is to a great degree considered responsible. When religious festivals take place, the sheiks meet and take the chief part in them, and if they are, as is very often the case, bigoted and ill-disposed to Christians, the feeling of all the village is bad, and surly replies and cold looks are apt to meet our efforts to get a friendly reception. If, however, the sheik be kind-hearted and easy, and still more if he be an intelligent, well-disposed man, we can quickly get listeners to our Master's message. Of course I do not mean that *every thing* turns on one man, but he may be a great hindrance or a great help from his position. At one very large village, or rather a cluster of villages very near each other, we have several times met with kind and cheering receptions, and on my last visit, when I introduced

[1] Mr. Naseef, the present director of the boys' school, and lay missionary.

my younger companions, who had not been on the river before, to some of my former village friends, the way in which all were welcomed was very pleasant. The sheik, a man of considerable intelligence, urged us to come to his house, and sat in the "salamlik," or outer room reserved for men, with Mr. Naseef and a few friends, conversing on the subject of religion, and bringing forward his objections and difficulties in a friendly spirit, while I went to the court, with two or three little dens opening into it; this answered to a harem, and here Miss Naseef and I were received by his wife and mother; the wife was busy churning butter in a skin, but came forward very cordially to salute us, and then continued her occupation, while we conversed with the old mother, a bright, intelligent-looking person, who, in spite of her advanced years, had the year before made the long and fatiguing journey to Mecca. The pilgrimage is made partly on the Red Sea, which is said to be generally very rough, and partly on camel-back, over burning plains of sand, and to a native Egyptian, used to a quiet life among the palm-trees and clover-fields near the river, it must have been a most trying expedition. But the poor old dame was in *earnest*, and really thought it would please God and cleanse her from sin to visit what they think such a holy place. It would not have been wise to say any thing to hurt her feelings about pilgrimages in a first visit (for though I had formerly seen the sheik, I had not known his mother), but we read and talked with her, and tried to show something of the plan of salvation through the atonement of the Saviour. When we took leave, the sheik accompanied us great part of the way, and when we were returned to our boat, after several more visits in other parts of the village, he sent his little son to ask for the copy of St. John's Gospel which he had been promised, and the child evidently had been told to take the greatest care of the book, for he trotted off holding it tightly to his breast with both his little hands.

Nearly all our store of books and tracts were taken at this place, and we did not leave without a promise, if the Lord should permit, to come again next year.

But we are not always so well received. At another village we found great hindrances. While Mr. Naseef was gone to fine the master of the little native school (a young man who gave instructions in reading and writing, their Koran being the *only* book used), his sister and I, in spite of an inconveniently high wind, tried to get up an acquaintance with some of the troop of women and girls who were loitering about; except one or two, who, from the noise like *slapping* which proceeded from their dwellings, were engaged, we knew, in bread-making, none seemed to be at all busy, and though many were very dirty and untidy, we saw many intelligent faces, as well as some very pretty ones, although that was of no consequence, as our business was with the *inside*. Some answered civilly, others stared and laughed rather rudely, others were silent, and looked sullen. At last one invited us to sit in an open court, where there was a raised seat or ledge of stone and mud against a wall, which somewhat sheltered us from the wind. A good number now assembled to hear what these strange ladies had to say, and what they wanted, which we were very glad to explain. I observed that they seemed to have fine corn land and beautiful date-trees in their place. "Oh, yes," said one women, "and fine goats,—look!" pointing to a flock just going to the pasture. "You have then most of you bread enough, but if you had none, and were nearly starving, and I had a basketful of loaves in my hand, would not you think me very hard-hearted if I did not give you some? and do not you think I would give it?" "Yes, certainly," said one, clapping me on the shoulder. "Well, I could only *offer* it,—if you refused I could not make you eat it, but hungry people are always glad of bread. But there is another kind of hunger, which we sometimes do not know when we have it. If we know scarcely any thing of God, and do not know how to please Him, nor where our souls can go when we die, then we are like starving people, only that it is the soul and not the body that wants food."

Then, after a few more simple words of explanation, I asked Miss Naseef, the lady who was with me, and who used to teach in my school in Cairo, to read a simple story from the Gospel, which she did, but it was hardly finished when we began to be annoyed by some boys, who had joined the women, and, getting on the seat behind us, began leaning on our shoulders, which was disagreeable, as they were in "filthy garments," but what was worse, they quarrelled and pushed each other, and talked loud, so that we could scarcely get a hearing any longer, and one of the men seemed inclined to speak very rudely.

Some of them were scholars in the little Mohammedan school, but *manners* were not taught there; indeed, a couple of hours early in the day was all the time they spent in school, we were told. More women pressed into the court now to see what was going on, and, to our dismay, some men with them. The men and women mix more freely and are more simple in their ways in the country villages than in town, but to *teach* a mixed party is hardly possible,—the women will never answer any question if men are present, and the men ask hard questions, or such as are evidently only put to try and puzzle or annoy the lady; so at least it was in this place, where the sheik was doubtless a very stiff and bigoted man. One of the men brought a great book, old and yellow, and written all by hand, and said, "If you want to read, read *that*,—there is a really good book." I replied I was not accustomed to that character (which is very unlike the printed books, and requires special study), and besides that, I only came to speak to the women, for whom the plain simple words of God's own Book, of which I had with me a portion, called the Gospel, was more suitable.

"Ah ha!" said one of them rudely, "your book,—does it say if it is a sin or not to eat pig's flesh?"

I told him as shortly as possible that Moses' law forbade this food to the Jews, who were to be separate not in that only, but many things, from all other people, but that the Gospel left people free about their food, and spoke of the spiritual matters, which are of more importance, adding that we begged they would permit us to read about the love of God, His mercy and His truth, rather than to engage in talk "which our friends here cannot enter into." "Yes, yes," said the man who had brought the book, in a very rough manner, and with a contemptuous smile, "read to the women, they are donkeys," and he turned away. A great many of the women, afraid of offending him (he was, I afterwards found, one of the chief men of the village), rose and went away.

We decided it was best to break up the assembly, and said we would go, as they did not care for God's word, but if any *did*, we would read to them in the fields quietly; then, pushing our way through the crowd, we got into an open corn-field not far off, and sat down under a beautiful palm-tree. Several young girls had followed us, and a few children, and one of the women. We made a circle here, and all promised to be quiet if we would read to them, and we had a very pleasant time with the young people. One girl especially interested us; her extreme intelligence was shown by the expression of her face. She was a sweet-looking girl, and seemed really glad to hear the new things we told of the Great and All-wise God condescending to love poor sinners, and sending His Holy One to die for them. One of the boys also showed a good deal of intelligence in his answers to the questions we put to him. What surprised us a good deal was to perceive that two or three of the men who had so troubled us had followed at a distance, and remained within ear-shot, but behind the group we were reading to, without uttering a word, or in any way troubling us. Perhaps some day we may find that a little seed has fallen on good ground, even in that village, which is marked in my journal as, "People bigoted and inclined to be rude."

Sometimes it is disappointing not to be able to find again some person who appeared to have been really touched and anxious to know more about Jesus. There was one such case, a widow woman, who had shown a remarkable sense of *sin* (I say remarkable, because, hard as it is everywhere to get the heart of man to acknowledge its sinfulness, it is hardest of all among Mohammedans). I sought for that woman vainly three years running, and never could trace where she had gone. There was also a very interesting Bedouin woman, who once had a long talk with me, and was deeply moved. She said,—I well remember her words, and the tear glistening in her bright black eye as she spoke,—"I am going away; we Bedouins move from place to place, and it may be years, perhaps, before I come to this spot again. How shall I recollect what you tell me?" adding, "Why did no one ever tell me this before?"

I need hardly say I promised to pray for her, and begged her to ask of God light for her soul and pardon for her sins. Still it was a difficult case, never to be in the way of hearing any thing of that Gospel which in one hour *could* only be put very imperfectly before her. These, and many, many more such, are cases for very earnest prayer and much faith.

I will now tell you one blessed instance in which the seed was found again, not by the sower indeed, but by his companion in the work. Many years ago the elder Mr. Shakoor was on the banks of the Nile engaged in distributing books among the Copts (or native Christians), for the higher up the Nile the more numerous are the Copts, to a certain distance. He was asked for books by a young man who told him he liked reading very much, and found but few books in his village, and had come some considerable way to get books, hearing "a strange gentleman was selling books at the river." He had seen, and perhaps partly read, a New Testament, but knew little about it, and cared less. He would have like worldly books better, and though he bought a New Testament, and listened to the earnest words spoken to him by that dear servant of the Lord, he paid little attention; at least, they soon passed out of his mind, because spiritual things had no interest for him. He examined his purchase at home, but found it was printed differently from the old Copt Bible he had seen, which had no paragraphs or spaces between the printed portions, as our books and *modern* Arabic ones have. So he foolishly fancied it was an imperfect copy, and actually threw it in the bottom of an old box, and soon forgot all about it. Years passed away, and at length the Copt heard some friends speaking of the Bible, and how they had procured it at the mission of the Americans at Luxor, and some one spoke of it as a different but better-printed edition than the old Coptic one. Then his forgotten New Testament came into the man's mind, and with that remembrance the unknown friend who had so affectionately urged him to read it. He hastened to seek in his old chest, and found it safe. The words despised at the time came back to him, and he now began the study of God's word in earnest; it was blessed to his soul, and one day, when visiting Cairo, he came to our book-shop and learned how the sower of the seed had been called to "go up higher," where no doubt they will one day meet. Meantime he told the surviving brother that this precious book was his constant companion, and the guide of his life!

Letter XV
About the School

It is now time I should tell you something in *order* about the school which has been alluded to so often in my letters. I kept it for the end because I wished you first to know a little about the sort of people for whose children it was set up, as, without this, details of schools are very dry reading, and however glad we may be that the poor children are taught well, yet, if we know nothing about the nation from which they come, and their ways and habits, etc., we can feel very little interest. Some of you may possibly have read one or both of two little books I wrote some years back, to give accounts of what I saw of the people, as well as of my endeavor to help them with education; but as many, no doubt, have not met with these, I will, at the risk of repeating some things already known, give you just a slight sketch of the beginning. I came for change of air when in poor health (but not by any means an actual invalid) many years ago, meaning to spend five or six months; and I thought I might *start* a school for poor girls in Cairo; a beloved relative had kindly accompanied me, and a valued maid-servant made up the party. We took a small house in a native quarter in order to try and get scholars among the poor, and especially Moslems; although warned by all friends that Moslem girls *never* would come to a Christian, I resolved at least to try, asking the Lord for a blessing. A worthy Syrian woman was found, whose daughter, only thirteen, could read fairly; she herself could read pretty well in the Gospels, and both could sew. The whole of their rather large family was squeezed into the house to save them house-rent.

We then began to make our arrangements, and look for pupils; first we tried through the native servants, but I was ignorant of the ways of Egypt, or should never have supposed that a man could have any power to bring girls. Many, many difficulties were in the path indeed, among which was my small knowledge of Arabic, and my good matron knew about as much of English, and her little daughter the same. We got on very well however; she and I went out to look for our scholars in the lanes near the house. The poor women we spoke to had never, many of them, seen a European, for Cairo was not so full of strangers as now, and they (if foreigners) kept more to particular quarters. In the lanes just around my new dwelling were numbers of poor houses, and a little further a collection of actual *huts*, built against the old wall of the city, and with narrow paths between them; the only thoroughfare was the street, which went lengthways, and into which these little paths opened. The occupants of these places seldom left home except on a visit to the tombs, or on a wedding procession, etc., and if they ever saw a "Frangee," as they called Europeans, it was at a distance, riding a donkey, or in a carriage; as to one *talking* to them, and going among them to ask if they would send their little girls to school, it was quite a new idea. Several ran away, and the children were terrified, and cried, and hid themselves, and at the good matron's advice I left the European straw hat at the house, and put a scarf over the head, so as to resemble more nearly what they were used to in dress. *Now*, such a proceeding would be absurd, they are used enough to hats of all kinds, and many Syrian and Greek girls have taken to wear them, and even some few Copts; but I am writing of things fully eighteen years ago. Some of the women were friendly, others sullen, being bigoted Moslems, and disliking Christians; others laughed, and said, "Teach girls indeed! let them make bread: what more need they know!" A few said, "Teach sewing if you will, this is very good; let *books* alone." A few at last agreed to try, and after two or three days all was prepared in a very simple way at the house, and a few scholars came. My cousin was ill with a low fever, and could not help me, but my excellent maid brought the needles and thread, and, though only possessing a few Arabic words, made the most of these, and was a great assistance those first days, with her bright face and cheerful manners, *ramming* thimbles on fingers quite new to them, and cutting bits of calico to be stitched, etc. I opened school with the Lord's prayer, and then I and my little teacher taught texts, and the matron kept order, or tried to do so, for she had never kept school, and the wild *hut* children were very hard to keep quiet. By little and little a few more respectable ones came, and helped the others, as they knew what sitting still and doing as they were told *meant*, at least; after a month's labors, my cousin was well again, and often gave us a helping hand, and the number of scholars gradually rose to twenty, more sometimes, seldom less.

I will not repeat all the ups and downs of that four months' work; when the middle of May came, my cousin and I left, and the school was placed under another lady, as I did not then see that God intended me to live and work here, and family affairs made it hard to be at such a distance. But the poor matron's health failed, and she had to go, the lady was inexperienced in the East, and ignorant of the language, and moreover had no one near who took a *real* interest in the work, so she closed the school and returned to England, and then I decided to go out and "stick to it," as the boys say; so that autumn found me (this time alone, except for my faithful maid) in my old quarters; luckily the lease was not out, and I opened the house, and the children were soon found again, and were wild with joy at my return.

I found a teacher who was half Italian, half Syrian, and as I spoke Italian I could easily explain things to her. She was much cleverer than my good matron and her little girl, but then they were Protestants, and she was of the Greek Church, and knew next to nothing of the Bible; so I had to teach the Scripture daily myself, and to study Arabic very hard to keep ahead of my scholars. The excellent Christian missionary, Mr. Mansoor Shakoor[1] (from Syria, but working in Egypt, under an English society), had made my acquaintance that winter, and kindly gave me Arabic lessons, and besides this, he came whenever he could to examine the children and keep the teacher up to her business. So we got on nicely, and even when I was obliged to go to Europe for the summer, the school kept up tolerably under the teachers, though I found much to reform on my return next autumn. By Mr. Shakoor's advice I engaged his brother, also a missionary teacher, to leave Syria and come as my agent to Cairo, to manage the business of the house with the landlord, and many other matters, and also to teach the Gospel to any among men or boys who could be persuaded to hear.

[1] The same alluded to as a fellow-worker in the last chapter, whose wife was my adopted daughter.

By degrees the work enlarged from this time, and after a while the elder Mr. Shakoor gave up his other situation and joined me, and the two Christian brothers, with one spirit and one heart, labored for the Lord,—opened meetings for young men, distributed Bibles, visited the sick, and at last arranged a boys' school. This was not easy, because we had scarcely funds to pay its expenses. I had carried on the work at my own expense, with only a very small amount of assistance from friends who were interested in it, and the yearly sum I could dispose of did not allow of such an addition. We tried, however, beginning by having the boys in a lower room in the house I occupied, the girls being already in an upper room, and God sent help, so that by and by we moved the boys to a larger house, and then again to another, till at last I was enabled to build a large school-house (with some assistance from Christian friends) on a plot of land presented to me by the Khedive, on which I also built a dwelling-house.

Many years of struggles and work had passed by this time, and we had had reason to praise the Lord for letting the little blade of corn grow and bring fruit and increase. Instead of twenty or thirty children, they came in fifties, and then in hundreds, and our rooms were full.

A younger brother, and afterwards other relatives, had come to join the Shakoors in their work, and by teaching in school left them more free for mission work with adults. The circle of laborers had one interest and one desire among them, and I was no longer alone in a strange land. A young relative of my first friend and helper, Mansoor Shakoor, had been spared by her parents at his earnest request to be an adopted daughter to me, and share my home and labors, and from an early age she gave herself to serve the Lord by trying to do good among the girls and women of Egypt.

Before the new school-house was built, this young lady and Mr. Shakoor were married, and the cares of a family prevented her going among the women as formerly, but much can be done at home, both by example and a word in season, and we had now quite an establishment of teachers and pupils, and old pupils and their relations coming to see us. In the evening the two missionaries took turns in holding meetings, and in winter (our best season, as I told you before) we made little voyages on the river, to bring the Gospel to some of the many villages on the coast, as related in the last letter.

Our work was prospering in many respects, though the bigotry of the people was the cause of frequent disappointment and much hindrance. Still God's word was preached as a testimony to many, and *some* listened gladly. The year that the building which with so much trouble we had at length finished was opened, was *the* year of sorrow to the Cairo mission; the elder Mr. Shakoor was called above, after a severe illness of more than two months. *Faith* can sometimes hear the Lord's welcome to the "good and faithful servant," but alas! too often faith even seems *dimmed* by tears. Yet God mercifully continued to uphold the work, as well as to support the bereaved.

A few years later, and the second brother, Mr. Joseph, was called away, like the first, having scarcely reached middle age, and leaving also a widow and little ones, who returned to Syria after his death.

Two years previous to this second blow, we had opened a branch school for boys in the ancient though decayed city of Damietta, on the coast of the Mediterranean, where one of the mouths of the Nile pours its waters into that sea. Mr. Joseph Shakoor had gone there to make the arrangements, as it was from an earnest request made to him from a few respectable inhabitants that the *idea* of opening a school there arose.

He started the work and took much interest in it, and his cousin, who had joined our little band some time before, was deputed to superintend the work in this untrodden field (for no missionary had ever taught God's word there before). The school is still doing well there, but the preaching, etc. was suspended for a time, except during the occasional short visits of the missionary, as on the death of Mr. J. Shakoor he was obliged to come to Cairo. But a missionary will, by God's help, soon be placed there.

You must not suppose that all who come to learn profit as fully as we wish, or that the children are open professors of Christianity. It would not be wise to *make* them, or even *urge* them, to come out while things are as they are in this country; the persecution any Mohammedan is sure to undergo if he is *baptized* a Christian would very likely frighten children into recanting, and they would be removed entirely from Gospel influence, while too weak to stand unassisted and alone. But their *belief* in the Gospel is not interfered with in general; they are left to do and think much as they like, and the degree of freedom often surprises me, and is cause of thanksgiving. In early days I had often dust thrown at me when visiting in the lanes, and many bad words and curses. These are now very, very rare, and though there is much *intense* bigotry still, there are yet small loopholes for light here and there, and the best and largest of these (indeed it is not a *small* loophole!) is the softening of the prejudice against education, and what is most wonderful, education by a Christian is still prized, and much more than formerly. Far from having to go and hunt for scholars, I am obliged to refuse taking more till there is space, large as our rooms are.

You would be pleased if you could see the gate of the school-house at twelve o'clock, when the bell rings, and out come the boys pouring in streams, all full of glee, some with books under their arms, others running to the fruit or sweetmeat seller at the door, others in little groups sitting under a beautiful mulberry-tree (planted the second year of the building of the great school-house), and others under a vine trellis, where a bench is provided, all enjoying the dinners they have brought, or which their mothers have sent. The greater number are poor boys still, but several are rich, and these have their meal brought by a black slave or a hired servant, in a covered dish. A few who live near go home to eat. About three hundred may usually be seen, this being the average attendance. 'The girls number two hundred; many more are on the books, but they are oftener kept away in cases of illness in the house,—new babies' arrivals, and other causes.

The girls have their playground quite separate, and on the other side of the house; their school-room is up-stairs, and the staircase is separate also. They have a number of teachers, the younger ones being all trained girls brought up by ourselves. One of the very best of these is sister to the dear girl whose blessed death I told you about, and I trust she has the same blessed hope. Though past the ridiculously early age at which girls are usually married, she is still a happy young teacher with us, and her mother says she will not let her Zeynab marry unless to a really good and respectable man, if she can find such.

The young lady who is over the school, and directs these young teachers, has been in England herself (though a native of Syria), and has seen English schools, and many of the good works going on in London, and tells the women here about them. You would like to see her seated in the school-room, with the whole school assembled in the morning, sitting quite still and in perfect order, listening while she reads a short portion of Scripture, and tries by questions to ascertain that all know what it is about, and to make the elder ones explain by their answers to the younger.

All ages, from fourteen to four or five, are there, and every sort of garment, from the muslin dress and handsome necklace of the wealthy child to the coarse calico loose frock, the only article of the poorest. But we discourage *finery* in school, and much less in the way of jewels, etc. are seen than was the case some time ago, even rich mothers being now persuaded that plain colored prints, or clean white in summer, are more suitable for the place and occupation, and the *cleanliness* enforced in all is now so thoroughly established that only a *new* comer now appears with face or hair or frock in an unpleasant state. Formerly I had the utmost trouble to get clean faces, and many mothers refused to give clean dresses, from fear of the evil eye; but this, among scholars at least, is now disappearing, and the fresh, clean look of the young assembly never fails to strike our visitors with pleasure.

Some of the very poorest receive a calico frock in winter, and need it very much, for several are orphans, and others children of widows, or *worse*,—of poor women divorced, and obliged to labor for themselves and little ones. If the child is a boy, the father always keeps it, but a girl, unless he is particularly fond of her, or wants her to wait on the new wife, is generally on the poor mother's hands. We think a few yards of calico well bestowed on such, and only wish we had more to give.

They are taught, after the Scripture (which is made the first object of all), some hymns, and the simplest part of arithmetic and geography, and some knowledge of English to the head class.

After school is dismissed, the pupil teachers generally stay half an hour later in the summer evenings to enjoy strolling in my garden, or sitting under a tree with their work. Sometimes a young married scholar (from the Syrians, who are not so closely shut up as Egyptians) joins them, and they always come on Sunday for our Arabic service in the school-house. All these are sweet, promising girls, and their mothers, most of whom are widows, are very proud of them.

But even among much younger ones we have scholars whose answers in Scripture are very good for their age, and down to the least every child who has been here for a month knows that Jesus Christ is the Saviour of sinners, and by Him alone we can hope for an entrance to heaven.

Many of the mothers of the children come to see the school and the teachers, and hear what is taught; some come to my little weekly women's meetings, though Eastern women dislike regularity and order so much that it is hard to get any of them to come steadily every week; yet more or less are there, and by degrees we hope to induce them to be steady attendants. Some days eighteen or twenty, and even as many as forty, will appear, at others only three or four; but usually at least seven or eight women will come, some Christians and some Moslems, and I read and pray with them, and try to explain the reading in a simple, cheerful manner, and to show how blessed a thing it is to believe in Jesus.

I visit many of them at their homes, and Mrs. Shakoor still more, for that is the part of the work she especially undertakes, and many of the Mohammedan women, whose children or *relations'* children attend school, have heard the

Gospel from her, and welcome her when she goes to see them, and Copts and Syrians as well.

Thus the school has opened doors which might *never* have been opened for the Gospel without it, for Egyptians are shy of receiving total strangers without some reason, and having their girls under our care was of course the best of reasons. That curtain which in Mohammedan families of the better class hangs before the entrances to the women's apartments is not so easily raised for foreign visitors as might be supposed; even ladies do not gain admission into many of them. We are let in, however, at once, as soon as known.

Not long ago I went to a house where the mistress is a bigoted woman, whom I often hear muttering sentences she has learned by heart (for she cannot read) of the Koran, and telling beads, which is not common among women, few of whom know much of their own religion, or perform the stated Moslem prayers as men do; yet this lady sends her little girl to the school (though they live at some distance), and not only receives us affectionately, but when I visited her lately she asked me if I had "that book" in my pocket, as if so she wished I would read a bit! I had the book, and very gladly complied with her request; she said, turning to a lady older than herself, who was a cousin, I believe, who was staying with her,—"My girl reads quite nicely in that book now,—yes, she is clever indeed."

I should make my letter too long were I to tell of the various *openings* made in different families by scholars, some very hopeful, others like a tiny chink in a closed door, just enough to let in a single ray of light; but we have cause to thank God and persevere, and say, as His people so often can say, "Hitherto hath the Lord helped us" (1 Samuel 7:12).

I must before leaving this subject give you a little *picture*, which I think will please you: it is our Sunday school in holiday-time. In the latter part of summer the teachers require a little rest; the parents of the scholars by no means like it, as the children are on their hands, and boys get into mischief; however, it cannot be helped for a little while. But I assembled as many as I could of the girls during the holidays on Sunday for a little meeting, something between a Sunday school and regular service. Only a few out of the number came, but we knew those came from their own free will,—from thirty to forty girls and the pupil teachers, and a few women, on the occasion I am describing here, in all thirty-two, made quite a group in the vine-covered arbor where I assembled them. After all the salutations were over, I opened with a short prayer, and then read the 16th of Acts, pausing for a question now and then, and at the end making a few remarks; some of the girls answered very intelligently, and all appeared interested. Then we had a hymn, and another prayer, and I then dismissed the assembly to refresh themselves in the garden, while I heard the verses learnt by the home-girls.[1] It was a pretty sight to observe the pupil teachers, tall girls of fifteen, with their modest, quiet manners and bright faces, and to hear their replies to questions about the chapter, and to remember how they used to come to my school when quite little toddlers; the women too seemed so calmly happy as they sat under the willow-tree, and talked with the matron while enjoying the fresh air, for they all lived in narrow lanes, which are in August quite suffocating, and the sun being nearly set, my shady garden was delightful to them. I thought how I wished they could know by blessed

[1] Some orphans I am bringing up in the house.

experience what it is to be able to say of the Lord Jesus, "I sat down under His shadow with great delight" (Song of Solomon 2:3). May that time come for them, and for you too, if you do not yet know it.

Letter XVI
Conclusion

And now, my dear friends, I must bid you farewell. I shall not think my trouble wasted if some of you have learned in reading these pages to feel a greater interest in Egypt than you ever did before, and, I hope, to feel also some interest in the people, and to ask the Lord to gather out of them a band of true believers, and to hasten that blessed time when Egypt shall be a *third* with Israel and Assyria (see Isaiah 19). We cannot understand fully the connection between our poor imperfect prayers and the plans of our Heavenly Father, but He has *told* us to pray not only for ourselves, but for others, and not only for individuals, but also for nations, and therefore I may boldly ask for your prayers both for the people of Egypt and for my little mission among them in particular. You know God's telegraph-wire never breaks: no fear that the humblest petition sent up from an honest believing heart will fail to reach the Lord, and to be in *some* way answered, not perhaps for long, not in the expected way very likely, but not lost. Let us then join in praying that the bread cast upon the waters may be found after many days, that the little ones whom I am trying to train up to know the Saviour may become His true disciples, and that He who is the "Dayspring from on high" (Luke 1:78) may give light to them that sit in darkness and the shadow of death, to guide their feet into the way of peace.